Football Quiz 1980/81

This Armada book belongs to:

_____

_____

_____

About the author

Gordon Jeffery has been, in his own words, 'fitba' daft'
from the age of eight. He is the author and editor of
many books on football as well as of countless articles,
reviews and stories on soccer and other sports, and he
even contributes to sporting papers in countries as far
afield as Australia and the Soviet Union. He acts as editorial
adviser each year to the *All Stars Annual,* and has written
previous football quiz books for Armada, as well as
*The Armada Cricket Quiz Book, The Armada Book of
Sporting Records* and *The Armada Book of the World Cup.*

He lives in Portsmouth, in Hampshire, where he is a loyal
supporter of Portsmouth F.C.

Football
Quiz 1980/81

by Gordon Jeffery

An Armada Original

On the cover: (Front) Kevin Keegan playing for England. (*By permission of Sporting Pictures.*) (Back) *Top:* Terry McDermott – Players' Player of the year 1979/80 – in action for Liverpool. *Bottom:* Young England player Glen Hoddle in action for Tottenham Hotspur against Nottingham Forest. (*By permission of Syndication International.*)

Football Quiz 1980/81
was first published in 1980 in Armada
by Fontana Paperbacks,
14 St. James's Place, London SW1A 1PS

Printed in Great Britain by
Love & Malcomson Ltd., Brighton Road,
Redhill, Surrey.

EUROPEAN FOOTBALL CHAMPIONSHIP 1979/80

Preliminary Round in 7 Qualifying Groups

Results and final tables

GROUP ONE

Home Team	Bulg.	Den.	Eng.	N.I.	R. of I.
Bulgaria	—	3–0	0–3	0–2	1–0
Denmark	2–2	—	3–4	4–0	3–3
ENGLAND	2–0	1–0	—	4–0	2–0
N. Ireland	2–0	2–1	1–5	—	1–0
Rep. of Ireland	3–0	2–0	1–1	0–0	—

	P	W	D	L	F	A	Pts.
ENGLAND	8	7	1	0	22	5	15
N. Ireland	8	4	1	3	8	14	9
Rep. of Ireland	8	2	3	3	9	8	7
Bulgaria	8	2	1	5	6	14	5
Denmark	8	1	2	5	13	17	4

GROUP TWO

	Aus.	Bel.	Nor.	Por.	Scot.
Austria	—	0–0	4–0	1–2	3–2
BELGIUM	1–1	—	1–1	2–0	2–0
Norway	0–2	1–2	—	0–1	0–4
Portugal	1–2	1–1	3–1	—	1–0
Scotland	1–1	1–3	3–2	4–1	—

	P	W	D	L	F	A	Pts.
BELGIUM	8	4	4	0	12	5	12
Austria	8	4	3	1	14	7	11
Portugal	8	4	1	3	10	11	9
Scotland	8	3	1	4	15	13	7
Norway	8	0	1	7	5	20	1

GROUP THREE

	Cyp.	Rum.	Spn.	Yugo.
Cyprus	—	1–1	1–3	0–3
Rumania	2–0	—	2–2	3–2
SPAIN	5–0	1–0	—	0–1
Yugoslavia	5–0	2–1	1–2	—

	P	W	D	L	F	A	Pts.
SPAIN	6	4	1	1	13	5	9
Yugoslavia	6	4	0	2	14	6	8
Rumania	6	2	2	2	9	8	6
Cyprus	6	0	1	5	2	19	1

GROUP FOUR

	E.G.	Ice.	Neth.	Pol.	Swtz.
East Germany	—	3–1	2–3	2–1	5–2
Iceland	0–3	—	0–4	0–2	1–2
NETHERLANDS	3–0	3–0	—	1–1	3–0
Poland	1–1	2–0	2–0	—	2–0
Switzerland	0–2	2–0	1–3	0–2	—

	P	W	D	L	F	A	Pts.
NETHERLANDS	8	6	1	1	20	6	13
Poland	8	5	2	1	13	4	12
East Germany	8	5	1	2	18	11	11
Switzerland	8	2	0	6	7	18	4
Iceland	8	0	0	8	2	21	0

GROUP FIVE

	Cze.	Fra.	Lux.	Swd.
CZECHOSLOVAKIA	—	2–0	4–0	4–1
France	2–1	—	3–0	2–2
Luxembourg	0–3	1–3	—	1–1
Sweden	1–3	1–3	3–0	—

	P	W	D	L	F	A	Pts.
CZECHOSLOVAKIA	6	5	0	1	17	4	10
France	6	4	1	1	13	7	9
Sweden	6	1	2	3	9	13	4
Luxembourg	6	0	1	5	2	17	1

GROUP SIX

	Fin.	Gre.	Hun.	USSR
Finland	—	3–0	2–1	1–1
GREECE	8–1	—	4–1	1–0
Hungary	3–1	0–0	—	2–0
U.S.S.R.	2–2	2–0	2–2	—

	P	W	D	L	F	A	Pts.
GREECE	6	3	1	2	13	7	7
Hungary	6	2	2	2	9	9	6
Finland	6	2	2	2	10	15	6
U.S.S.R.	6	1	3	2	7	8	5

GROUP SEVEN

	W.G.	Mal.	Tur.	Wal.
WEST GERMANY	—	8–0	2–0	5–1
Malta	0–0	—	1–2	0–2
Turkey	0–0	2–1	—	1–0
Wales	0–2	7–0	1–0	—

	P	W	D	L	F	A	Pts.
WEST GERMANY	6	4	2	0	17	1	10
Turkey	6	3	1	2	5	5	7
Wales	6	3	0	3	11	8	6
Malta	6	0	1	5	2	21	1

Final Tournament in Italy

(Group winners qualify for the FINAL; runners-up contest 3rd/4th places. If level on points goal-difference decides. If goal-difference is the same, higher number of goals scored decides.)

GROUP ONE

11 June	Rome	Czechoslovakia	0	West Germany	1
11 June	Rome	Czechoslovakia	0	West Germany	0
11 June	Naples	Netherlands	1	Greece	1
14 June	Rome	Czechoslovakia	3	Greece	1
14 June	Naples	West Germany	3	Netherlands	2
17 June	Milan	Czechoslovakia	1	Netherlands	1
17 June	Turin	West Germany	0	Greece	0

	P	W	D	L	F	A	Pts.
1. WEST GERMANY	3	2	1	0	4	2	5
2. Czechoslovakia	3	1	1	1	4	3	3
3. Netherlands	3	1	1	1	4	4	3
4. Greece	3	0	1	2	1	4	1

GROUP TWO

12 June	Turin	Belgium	1	England	1
12 June	Milan	Italy	0	Spain	0
15 June	Milan	Belgium	2	Spain	1
15 June	Turin	Italy	1	England	0
18 June	Naples	Spain	1	England	2
18 June	Rome	Italy	0	Belgium	0

	P	W	D	L	F	A	Pts.
1. BELGIUM	3	1	2	0	3	2	4
2. Italy	3	1	2	0	1	0	4
3. England	3	1	1	1	3	3	3
4. Spain	3	0	1	2	2	4	1

3rd/4th places

21 June Naples Italy 1 Czechoslovakia 1
   CZECHOSLOVAKIA won on penalties 9–8.

FINAL

22 June Rome WEST GERMANY 2 Belgium 1
   (Hrubesch 2) (Vandereycken)

1. European Club Badges—1

Below are the badges of six clubs who played against English clubs in one or other of the European club competitions in the 1979/80 season. With the exception of the Swedish club at D, it should be fairly easy to (a) name each club and its country. Can you also remember (b) which English club each played against, (c) in which competition, and (d) with what aggregate result? (Simply won or lost—not the actual scores.)

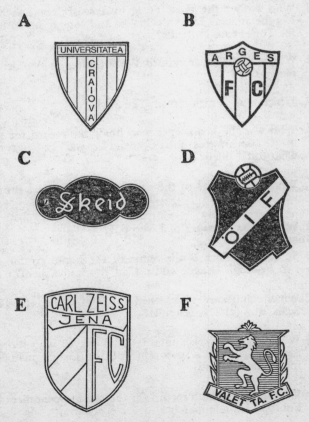

2.   Ready for the Kick-Off?

Here to warm up before tackling the rest of the puzzles and quizzes are a dozen quick questions, and, I hope, quick answers!

1. Which club plays its home matches at Old Trafford?

2. Terry Venables is the manger of which club?

3. Who scored the most goals in a season in Football League matches for both Chelsea and, later in his career, for Tottenham Hotspur?

4. Who was the most capped Wolverhampton Wanderers player?

5. Which club is nicknamed 'The Posh'?

6. Who was the goalkeeper who holds the record for the most appearances in Football League matches for Charlton Athletic?

7. What is the name of the home ground of West Bromwich Albion?

8. Who is the manager of Liverpool?

9. St. James's Park is the name of the home ground of two Football League clubs. Can you name them?

10. Which clubs are nicknamed (a) The Gulls, (b) The Seals, and (c) The Seagulls?

11. Who was the Welsh international player who scored the most goals in a season in Football League matches for Leeds United?

12. Who holds the club record for the most appearances in Football League matches for Liverpool?

3. Between the Sticks

From the picture clues can you work out the names of these six goalkeepers? Two of them have been 'capped' many times; two of the others are experienced players whilst the remaining two are newcomers to the 'big-time'.

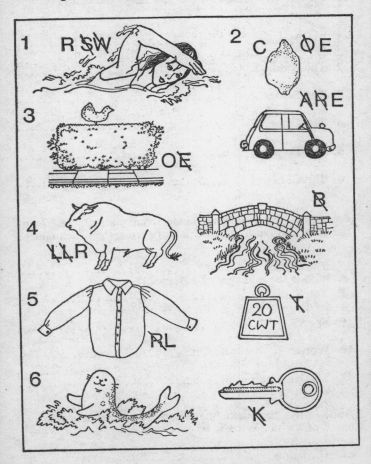

4. Nicknames

Nearly every football club has a nickname. Often the nicknames are nearly as old as the clubs themselves and they derive from the main industry or craft of the town when the local professional football club was founded. Here are some examples—can you name the clubs?

1. The Hatters ....

2. The Saddlers ....

3. The Blades ....

4. The Gunners ....

5. The Potters ....

6. The Cobblers ....

Sometimes the nicknames come from the actual name of the club. Can you name these clubs from their nicknames?

7. The Dons ....

8. The Shots ....

9. Spurs ....

10. Wolves ....

11. The Hammers ....

And, lastly, the nickname below comes from an earlier name of a club. What is its present name?

12. The Saints ....

5. Seven for England

With the help of the clues below, can you fill in the names of the seven England players? All have played for England in recent seasons.

					E			
1	C	O	P	P	E	L	L	
2		B	A	R	N	E	S	
3		K	E	E	G	A	N	
4		S	H	I	L	T	O	N
5			W	A	T	S	O	N
6	C	H	A	N	N	O	N	
7	W	O	O	D	D	C	O	C	K

1. Liverpool-born but soon spotted by Manchester United when playing for Tranmere Rovers and brought to Old Trafford. He scored the only goal of the match against Scotland at Hampden Park in 1978.
2. The winger son of a wing-half who, like his father before him, played for Manchester City. But our player was transferred to West Bromwich Albion in the 1979/80 season.
3. The heart and the head of many recent England teams who is coming home from West Germany to lead England's challenge for the 1982 World Cup.
4. One of probably the world's best two goalkeepers—and both of them are English!
5. The big defender who left Manchester City for Werder Bremen but soon returned to England to play for Southampton.
6. First capped when a Saint in 1972, moved to Manchester City in 1977—and added only one more to his 40-odd "caps" when with them! Came home to the Dell in 1979.
7. The third current English international player to take the trail to West Germany—in his case from Nottingham Forest to Cologne.

6. An Anagram Eleven

During all or part of the 1979/80 football season the eleven players whose anagrammed names are shown below played in countries that were foreign to them—one of them, by the way, soon returned to his home country. Can you (a) unravel their names, (b) say for which foreign (to them) club they played and (c) from which home country and club they came?

BEAT POOR ART   ....

GI COAL VAN   ....

SAVE TON WAD   ....

JANS FRESH TINS   ....

HARD RUN LEMON   ....

OLD LIAR VICAR   ....

GAVE KEEN KIN   ....

AX LABEL ALES   ....

MAKE EAR DIZZY IN   ....

A LAD DRIVES SOLO   ....

HUNG IN ANIMAL CURE   ....

7. In the Net

The letters making up the surnames of all the goalkeepers who have appeared for England and Scotland in the final stages of World Cup competitions are in the "net" drawn below. Every letter is used once but only once—so cross out each one as you use it. Below are listed the years of the competitions but remember that *both* countries were not in the final stages every time. When the same keeper appeared in more than one final stage, his name is only included once.

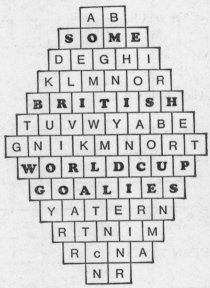

	England	Scotland
1950	....	....
1954	....	....
1958	....	....
1962	....	....
1966	....	....
1970	....	....
1974	....	....
1978	....	....

8. A Winning Team

In 1979 Nottingham Forest won the European Champion Clubs Cup by beating Malmo 1–0. Can you, using every square, fill in the name of Forest's winning team in the diagram below?

9. Last Season in the Football League

1. Who, after 50 seconds, scored the first goal in the 1979/80 Football League season? For which club?

2. Most unusually, one of the First Division matches due to be played on the opening day of the season was postponed. Which match and why was it postponed?

3. Brighton, in the First Division for the first time in their history, were beaten 4–0 at home in their opening match. By which club?

4. There were no hat-tricks in the First Division on the opening day but two black players scored twice. One of them for (a) Norwich and the other for (b) Stoke. Can you name the players?

5. By the end of the season Birmingham City were challenging for promotion whilst Fulham struggled to avoid relegation but it looked different at the beginning of the season when, after being 0–3 down at half-time at Birmingham, Fulham won 4–3. Who scored a hat-trick for the London club?

6. Which was the last club in the Football League last season to lose their 100% record?

7. Which were the last clubs to lose their *unbeaten* records last season in (a) the First Division and (b) the Football League as a whole?

8. Which club on 17 November 1979 ended Nottingham Forest's run of 49 First Division matches at home without defeat? And what was remarkable about Forest's defeat?

9. David Johnson was injured playing for England against the Republic of Ireland and missed Liverpool's game the following Saturday. Who replaced him and scored a hat-trick?

10. Who came on as substitute to make his first appearance in a Football League match and with his first *kick* (he had earlier *headed* the ball) scored for Southampton against Manchester City?

10. If you were the Referee—1

Imagine that you are the referee in a match when the incident shown below occurs—the goalkeeper with a late dive has just been able to stop the ball. But was he in time? Do you award a goal or not? If not, why not?

11. A Good Day for the Home Clubs

As the scores of the First Division matches in the Spanish League listed below started coming through from the Press Agencies, it seemed that on the day, either the defences were having a poor day or the striking forwards were on their best form! The first four results of the matches listed produced six, seven, three and seven goals respectively with every team scoring and Rayo Vallecano with five goals out on their own as the day's top-scorers.

However, after that rush of high-scoring matches, goals became scarcer with six teams failing to score. Those that did score, though, all did so more than once. Real Sociedad were the day's only away winners, whilst the spectators at Barcelona's match saw the only drawn game.

Given that the total number of goals scored in the nine matches came to 31, can you fill in the scores?

Las Palmas	... ...	Atletico Madrid	... ...
Athletic Bilbao	... ...	Seville	... ...
Valencia	... ...	Malaga	... ...
Rayo Vallecano	5 ...	Burgos	2 ...
Barcelona	... ...	Gijon	... ...
Almeria	... ...	Hercules	... ...
Zaragoza	... ...	Real Sociedad	... ...
Betis	... ...	Salamanca	... ...
Real Madrid	... ...	Espanol	... ...

12.   A Riddle to Solve

The first name and the surname of a well-known footballer can be discovered in this little riddle.

My first is in KERNEL but not in NUT,

My second's in KNIFE but not in CUT.

My third is in VAIN but not in PROUD,

My fourth is in NOISE but not in LOUD,

My fifth is in CHANT that you hear from the CROWD.

My first is in KICK but not in BALL,

My second's in LEAP but not in FALL.

My third is in SQUARE but not in ROUND,

My fourth is in GOAL and also in GROUND.

My fifth is in ALSO and also in AND,

The last makes my NAME and I captain ENGLAND!

Who am I?

13. Players on the Move

The 1978/79 Football League season saw the first transfer of a player's registration at a cost of a million pounds—that of Trevor Francis's from Birmingham to Nottingham Forest. But there were many other transfers before the deadline at 5 p.m. on the 29th March. Can you remember these?

1. Who was the player whose transfer fee was a record for that of a goal-keeper? Which club sold and which one bought?

2. A British record was also set for the transfer of a full-back. Who was he? From which club was he transferred? Who welcomed him as a new boy?

3. Middlesbrough (a) sold a player to West Bromwich Albion for over half a million pounds and (b) bought a winger from Burnley. Can you name the players concerned?

4. Leicester were rebuilding their side and sold (a) a back to Sunderland and (b) a central defender to Watford. Can you name them?

5. Wrexham transferred (a) a midfield player to Manchester United and (b) bought a back from Liverpool? Who were they?

6. Tottenham (a) bought a Scottish back from Aston Villa and (b) sold a Scottish midfield player to Bolton. Can you name them?

The last day for the transfer of registrations of players in time for them to play in the remaining Football League matches of the season brought the usual rush of business. This included—

7. An exchange of two forwards, each valued at £280,000, between Everton and Queen's Park Rangers. Which two players?

8. A Polish player from Legia Warsaw joining Bolton Wanderers. Can you name him?

9. Sheffield Wednesday acquiring a former Nottingham Forest and Derby County winger from Southampton. His name is?

10. The arrival at Goodison Park of a former star forward of Manchester United, Arsenal and Manchester City. Who was he?

14. Cup and League Champions

The names of two famous English clubs are coded in the puzzle. Can you crack the code and name them? What record does each club hold in relation to the F.A. Cup in one case, and the Football League Championship in the other?

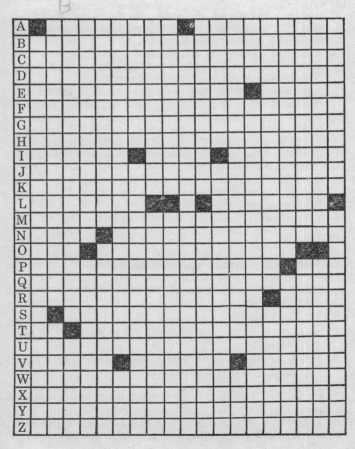

15. England's Road Back

1. In June 1979 England toured Bulgaria (for a European Football Championship qualifying match), Sweden and Austria. With what results? (Win, draw or lose if you cannot remember the actual scores.)

2. What did the match against Sweden celebrate?

3. In the 1979 British Home Championship which two of the four countries were unbeaten?

4. In England's team for the match against Wales in the 1979 British Home Championship there were two new "caps". One of the newcomers was a Crystal Palace player and the other then with West Bromwich Albion. Can you name them?

5. Who scored England's only goal in their 1–0 win over Denmark and both goals when they defeated the Republic of Ireland 2–0? Both of these EFC qualifying group matches were played at Wembley.

6. Who could not remain in England to play against Bulgaria when fog postponed the match for a day?

7. Who was (a) the already selected new "cap" who scored in that match and (b) the new "cap" who replaced the unavailable player of the previous question?

8. Bryan Robson of West Bromwich Albion made his first appearance for England in a Full International match in February 1980. Against which country?

9. England's last match in the EFC qualifying competition was at Wembley against the Republic of Ireland. (a) David Johnson (England) and (b) the Irish goalkeeper both had to go off after a clash of heads. Who replaced them?

10. England dropped only one point in their eight matches in the European Football Championship qualifying competition. In which match were they held to a draw and where was that match played?

16. Foreign Clubs with English Names

These badges are interesting because they remind us that it was Britishers who introduced football to many foreign countries. They are the badges of foreign clubs with English names or, as in D, the English spelling of a foreign place. Three of the clubs are European and three are South American. The initials CAR, SBA and YB stand for Club Always Ready, Sporting Boys Association and Young Boys. In C and D the obvious "give-away" place-names have been blacked out. Can you name the six clubs and say in which cities and countries they are at home?

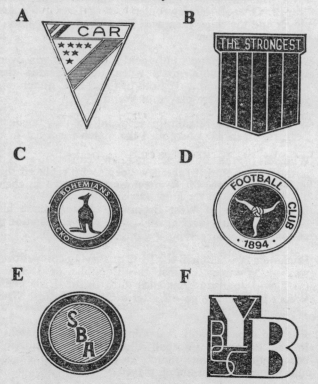

17. True or False?

Can you say which of the following statements are true and which are false? If you think they are false—why?

1. In England's World Cup qualifying match against Italy at Wembley in November 1977, four players, Barnes, Coppell, Latchford and Wilkins, made their first appearances in a Full International match.

2. During the first half of the 1977/78 season, which ended with Liverpool winning the European Champion Clubs Cup for the second year in succession, the Anfield team got only two points from a succession of five First Division matches.

3. Martin Peters was the only footballer playing in Football League matches in the 1979/80 season to have scored 20 or more goals for England in Full International Matches.

4. Everton in 1932, Tottenham in 1951, Ipswich in 1962 and Nottingham Forest in 1978, are the only clubs to have won the Football League Championship in the season immediately after the one in which they were promoted to the First Division.

5. In the 1978/79 season Everton were unbeaten in their first 19 matches in the First Division.

6. Only two members of Southampton's 1976 F.A. Cup winning team were in the Saints' team beaten in the 1979 F.L. Cup Final. Oddly the two were the scorers of Southampton's goals in the latter match.

7. Following in Kevin Keegan's footsteps, Tony Woodcock was the next current English international player to be transferred to a West Germany club.

8. Oldham Athletic, Bristol City and Charlton Athletic have all been the runners-up (the second-placed club in other words) for the Football League Championship.

18. A Coded Sentence

Can you solve this coded sentence with the help of the given letters in the table below? You may be able to guess some of the letters after you have inserted the given ones in the top diagram. If you do, fill in also the number below the letter in the table below and this will help you to work out the sequence in the table.

When you have solved the puzzle, can you answer the question?

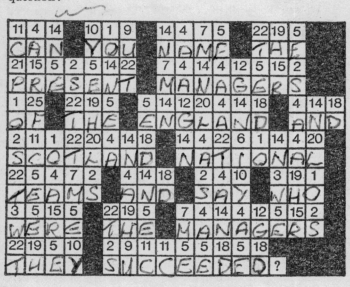

11	4	14		10	1	9		14	4	7	5			22	19	5
C	A	N		Y	O	U		N	A	M	E			T	H	E
21	15	5	2	5	14	22		7	4	14	4	12	5	15	2	
P	R	E	S	E	N	T		M	A	N	A	G	E	R	S	
1	25		22	19	5		5	14	12	20	4	14	18		4	14	18
O	F		T	H	E		E	N	G	L	A	N	D		A	N	D
2	11	1	22	20	4	14	18		14	4	22	6	1	14	4	20	
S	C	O	T	L	A	N	D		N	A	T	I	O	N	A	L	
22	5	4	7	2		4	14	18		2	4	10		3	19	1	
T	E	A	M	S		A	N	D		S	A	Y		W	H	O	
3	5	15	5		22	19	5		7	4	14	4	12	5	15	2	
W	E	R	E		T	H	E		M	A	N	A	G	E	R	S	
22	19	5	10		2	9	11	11	5	5	18	5	18				
T	H	E	Y		S	U	C	C	E	E	D	E	D	?		

A	B	C	D	E	F	G	H	I	J	K	L	M
			18									

N	O	P	Q	R	S	T	U	V	W	X	Y	Z
14	1				2							

19. Going to the Park?

In the years before the Second World War when most
people worked on Saturday mornings, at around eleven
o'clock during the football season you could be certain to
hear men asking their mates: "Going up to the match this
afternoon?" Or, in the case of the supporters of many of
the Football League clubs, "Going to the Park this afternoon?"

Below are some of the clubs whose home ground is a
"Park". How many of the clubs can you name?

1. Ayresome Park ....

2. Blundell Park ....

3. Elm Park ....

4. Ewood Park ....

5. Fellows Park ....

6. Goodison Park ....

7. Ninian Park ....

8. Prenton Park ....

9. Roker Park ....

10. Somerton Park ....

11. Springfield Park ....

12. Vale Park ....

20. National Flags to Colour

The national flags of four of the five countries that have won the European Football Championship (or the European Nations Cup as it used to be called) between 1960 and 1976 inclusive are shown in outline form. Firstly, can you identify the countries? Then, secondly, what are the colours?

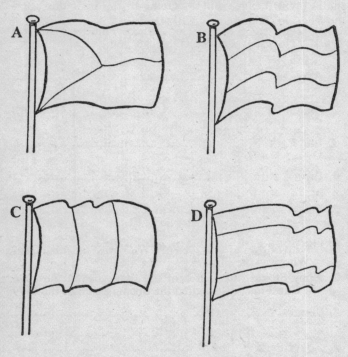

21. North American Way

The prominent part that British players are playing in the steadily increasing interest in football (or soccer as the North Americans call it to avoid confusion with their own American football game) that we noticed in the 1978/79 Football Quiz Book has continued. How much do you know about the game in North America?

1. What do the initials NASL stand for?

2. Probably the best known NASL club is New York Cosmos—but they do not play their home matches in either the city or the state of New York! Where do they play them?

3. Players with Football League clubs can be either transferred on a full-time basis to NASL clubs or loaned to them for their March–September season. What is the maximum number of players a F.L. club can release on loan to NASL clubs?

4. You will note from the previous question that the English and the North American seasons do overlap. From which club did Trevor Francis return with an injury that added to the number of Nottingham Forest matches he missed at the start of the 1979/80 season?

5. Another player, according to his F.L. club manager, delayed his return from the U.S.A. because he wanted to visit Elvis Presley's grave. (a) Who was the manager? (b) Who was the player?

6. Bobby Stokes, the scorer of the only goal in the 1976 F.A. Cup Final, also scored the opening goal of the 1979 NASL season. For which club did he score in (a) the Cup Final and (b) the NASL opening match?

7. Who was the former England player with Manchester City who was transferred full-time to New York Cosmos intending to finish his career in the U.S.A. but who was transferred back to Manchester City for £150,000 in January 1980?

8. Several players who had been prominent in the 1978 World Cup finals were signed by NASL clubs for their 1979 season. For which three NASL clubs did these five play? (a) Teofilio Cubillas and Gerd Muller; (b) Francisco Marinho and Eskandarian; and (c) Bjorn Nordqvist.

22. Six in the First

Can you identify these six Football League First Division players from the picture clues?

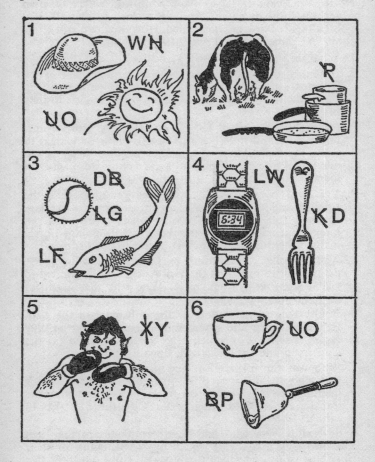

23. Name the Players

1. In Tottenham's replayed F.A. Cup tie against Manchester United at Old Trafford last season, who took over in goal when the injured Milija Aleksic had to come off?

2. Who was the player on loan to Nottingham Forest who scored the only goal of the first leg match against Barcelona in the 1980 European Super Cup?

3. Who was the Argentinian player transferred from the Spanish club Hercules Alicante to Sheffield United?

4. Stafford Rangers beat Kettering 2–0 at Wembley in the 1979 F.A. Challenge Trophy final. (a) Stafford's goalkeeper and (b) a Kettering striker were transferred to Football League clubs for the 1979/80 season. Can you name the players and the F.L. clubs for which each signed?

5. Who was the Welsh international player transferred from Middlesbrough to Swansea City in July 1979? What relation is he to the Swansea manager, John Toshack?

6. In January 1980 the first Mecca awards were presented. In future these will be for players completing 200, 300, 400 or 500 Football League games for a single club but, with one exception, the first eight awards were to former long-serving players. Below I have listed the top four with their clubs and number of appearances. Can you name them?
   (a) .... (Portsmouth 764 app.)
   (b) .... (Port Vale 761)
   (c) .... (Swindon 756)
   (d) .... (Southampton 713)

7. Fifth on the list of long-serving players was one still playing regularly for a London club. Can you name him?

8. Who at the end of 1979 was the European Footballer of the year for the second season in succession?

24. A Decade of English Cup-Winners and Champions

On the map on the facing page are marked the home towns of all the clubs that have won either the Football League Championship or the F.A. Cup or both of them during the

Name of clubs in alphabetical order	F. L. Champions	F.A. Cup Winners
	1971	1971
	–	1979
	–	1970
	1972	–
	1975	–
	1970	–
	–	1978
	1974	1972
	1973	1974
	1976	–
	1977	–
	1979	–
	–	1977
	1978	–
	–	1976
	–	1973
	–	1975

seventies (1970/79). Can you write in on the map the names of the clubs and then complete the chart opposite? You will see from the spacing in the chart that some of the clubs were winners or champions in more than one of the ten seasons.

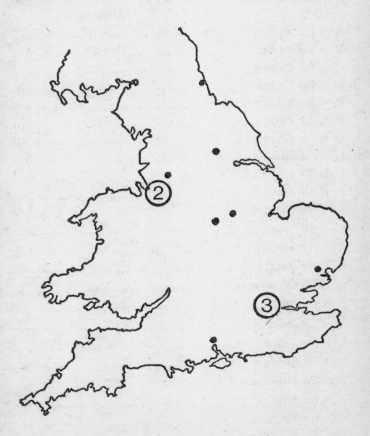

25. A World Cup A–Z

All the following players played in the 1978 World Cup
final tournament in Argentina. There is at least one player
from each of the 16 finalists. No player in the tournament
had a name beginning with either X or Y. Can you fill in
for which countries these played?

Country

A is for Ardiles ....

B is for Batista ....

C is for Cabrini ....

D is for Deyna ....

E is for Eskandarian ....

F is for Flohe ....

G is for Ghommidh ....

H is for Hickersberger ....

I is for Isiordia ....

J is for Janvion ....

K is for Kempes ....

L is for Leao ....

M is for Macari ....

N is for Neeskens ....

O is for Obermayer ....

P is for Pinter ....

Q is for Quiroga ....

R is for Rensenbrink ....

S is for Souness ....

T is for Tomaszewski ....

U is for Uria ....

V is for Vogts ....

W is for Wendt ....

Z is for Zoff ....

26. Close Encounters in Scotland

The same weekend during which the Italian League matches
shown in Puzzle No. 49 were played there was something
of the defensive Italian-look about the results of the five
Scottish League Premier Division matches played.

The five matches produced a total of eight goals scored
but no side could manage to score more than one goal.
The "old firm" clubs, Celtic and Rangers, gained the most
points from the encounters—and that information should
be enough for you to complete the scores of the matches
shown below.

Aberdeen .... Partick Thistle ....

Dundee .... Dundee United ....

Kilmarnock .... St. Mirren ....

Morton .... Celtic ....

Rangers .... Hibernian ....

27. In a Maze

By starting at the top left-hand square, and moving one square at a time in any direction, you can find the names and the clubs of three players in England's winning team against the Republic of Ireland in February 1980. Every letter is used but only once. Once you have got the solution you should be able to say what was unusual about the three playing for England in the match.

K	E	N	H	A	M	R	G
V	E	A	O	W	B	U	T
I	E	G	O	D	Y	N	O
N	K	R	U	A	C	O	C
E	I	A	■	D	L	E	K
C	U	M	D	R	I	N	C
N	I	L	A	E	R	G	O
N	N	G	H	A	M	O	L

28. A Mixed Bag

1. Who had set up a club record of 333 consecutive appearances before sustaining a shoulder injury that caused him to be replaced by the reserve keeper, Steve Ogrizovic?

2. Who in the late 1950s and early 1960s scored 251 goals in 271 Football League matches for Middlesbrough?

3. Who in the 1970s scored the winning goal for Everton in one Merseyside derby and for Liverpool in another one?

4. Who was the Englishman who scored 434 goals in Football League matches for various clubs, yet did not play in even one Full International match?

5. Who is the present-day Liverpool player with A-levels in History, English, Maths and Latin?

6. Who was the Englishman who managed the Malmo side that reached the Final of the European Champion Clubs Cup in 1979?

7. Who, playing in his first match in the European Champion Clubs Cup, scored the only goal in the 1979 Final of that competition?

8. Who scored a hat-trick for Wales against Scotland in the 1979 British Home Championship tournament?

9. Who scored a record of 60 goals in Football League matches in the season 1927/28 and died in March 1980 watching a Merseyside derby at Goodison Park?

10. Who, in December 1979, was released from his contract as the Welsh national team manager to become the manager of Hull City from 1st January 1980?

29. The Anglo-Scots

For over a hundred years Scottish footballers have come south of the border seeking bigger rewards for their skill than is generally to be obtained in Scotland. Between the two World Wars the Scottish F.A. used to arrange national team trials as matches between Home Scots and Anglo-Scots (meaning Scots with English clubs). Those matches have ceased but not the number of Anglo-Scots. Below are some of today's, with the name of the English club who brought them south. Can you write in from which Scottish club they came?

1. Aston Villa signed Andy Gray from ....

2. Leeds United signed Gordon McQueen from ....

3. Coventry City signed Garry Gillespie from ....

4. Liverpool signed Kenny Dalglish from ....

5. Aston Villa signed Allan Evans from ....

6. Manchester United signed Martin Buchan from ....

7. Middlesbrough signed Jim Stewart from ....

8. Newcastle United signed John Blackley from ....

9. West Ham United signed Ray Stewart from ....

10. Coventry City signed Ian Wallace from ....

11. Leeds United signed Joe Jordan from ....

12. Bristol City signed Tony Fitzpatrick from ....

13. Leeds United signed Derek Parlane from ....

14. Aston Villa signed Des Bremner from ....

15. Tottenham Hotspur signed Willie Young from ....

Something seems to have gone wrong in this copy of the teams sheet. Perhaps it was because of the excitement of the surprise victory of a Fourth Division club over a First Division one!

Can you complete the half-obliterated names of the players, say which two clubs they represented on the day, and what was the match and the result when the clubs played each other in January 1980?

KILNER	CORRIGAN
DUNLEAVY	RANSON
HUTT	POWER
EVANS	REID
HARRIS	CATON
HENDRIE	BENNETT
FIRTH	HENRY
KENNEDY	DALEY
MOUNTFORD	ROBINSON
SMITH	VILJOEN
STAFFORD	SHINTON

31. Of This and That

1. Only two men have managed two different Football League Championship winning clubs. Can you name them and the two winning clubs each managed?

2. On Easter Monday 1979, Aston Villa beat Liverpool 3-1 but in the full season (1978/79) Liverpool set up a new record for the least number of goals against in any division of the Football League. How many goals did Liverpool concede that season?

3. Managers are sacked and engaged so often that I have to word some questions very carefully. So, as at the last quarter of the 1979/1980 season who were the managers of (a) Sheffield Wednesday, (b) Doncaster Rovers and (c) Barnsley? And what is the connection between them?

4. Who was the Welsh international striker transferred from Swansea to Leeds United for £400,000 in May 1979?

5. Who was the West Bromwich Albion player transferred to Real Madrid in June 1979?

6. What was the result of the 1979 Charity Shield match played at Wembley?

7. In February 1979 Chelsea signed Eamonn Bannon from Hearts. To which Scottish club was he transferred later that year?

8. Who was appointed the Northern Ireland national team manager in February 1980 in succession to Danny Blanchflower?

9. Who was appointed the Welsh national team manager in March 1980 in succession to Mike Smith?

10. Who was officially appointed manager of Chelsea in October 1979 after a spell as the "caretaker" manager?

32. Up for the Cups

1. In the early rounds of the F.L. Cup, when the aggregated score from two legs is a draw and both clubs have scored the same number of goals, the U.E.F.A. idea of deciding the winners by successful penalty kicks has been introduced. Last season (a) a First Division club, after losing 0–2 at home in the second leg to a Third Division club, won on penalties and (b) a north-east derby tie was also decided by penalties. Which were the winning and losing clubs in those two ties?

2. In the Fourth Round of the F.L. Cup both (a) Wolverhampton Wanderers and (b) Nottingham Forest needed replays to progress after being held to one-all draws. By which clubs?

3. Which Third Division club knocked Everton out of the F.L. Cup in the Fourth Round?

4. In the First Round of the F.A. Cup (a) Crewe and (b) Oxford United were beaten by non-Football League clubs. Who were they?

5. Can you name the non-Football League club who knocked out both Southend and Leicester in the 1980 F.A. Cup?

6. In the Third Round of the 1980 F.A. Cup, (a) Newcastle to a Third Division club and (b) Chelsea to a Fourth Division club were each beaten at home? Which were the winning clubs?

7. Which clubs did (a) Nottingham Forest and (b) Wolverhampton Wanderers beat in the two-legged semi-finals of the 1980 F.L. Cup?

8. By contrast to their F.L. Cup progress, Wolves were beaten 0–3 at home to a lowly-placed Second Division club in the Fifth Round of the F.A. Cup. Who beat them?

9. A last-minute penalty goal, the only goal of the match, ended Aston Villa's interest in the 1980 F.A. Cup in the Sixth Round. Who was the scorer and for which club?

10. Who scored the only goal of the match in the 1980 Football League Cup Final at Wembley? For which club?

33. If You were the Referee—2

It is kick-off time. You, the referee, have looked across to see that your linesmen are ready and in position; checked your watches; and signalled for play to commence. Then, as the drawing below shows, the stripe-shirted centre-forward plays the ball back to a team-mate who immediately sends a long pass towards the touch-line to his right. A familiar opening move but are you, the referee, satisfied with it?

34. Coming Home

One of the hazards or, in some cases, one of the rewards of a professional footballer's career is that of being transferred to another club in a different part of the country—often at very short notice. Yet it is surprising that amongst all the to-ing and fro-ing, several players eventually come back to their old clubs. Here are some for you to identify.

1. After nearly 400 Football League appearances (and more than 150 goals) for his first (near home) club, he was transferred to Manchester City but after two seasons came back to his first south-country club.

2. Welsh international winger who began with Burnley and went on to Derby County and Queen's Park Rangers before returning to Burnley.

3. This powerful central defender born in Hornchurch played over a hundred league matches with Orient before coming to prominence with West Ham for whom he played more than 300 matches before returning to Orient in May 1979.

4. It was a fairly quick return home for this West country striker who returned to Exeter City in March 1980, fifteen months after being transferred by City to Blackpool.

5. This English international player stayed longer with Everton before returning to Burnley in August 1979. He had played in over 200 league matches for Burnley before joining Everton.

6. This one is not quite a return to a first club because this sturdy little forward had played a few matches for Nottingham Forest before moving to Walsall to score 125 goals in 241 league matches. He was then transferred to Birmingham City but within a year returned to Walsall as player-manager.

7. Popular Sunderland-born goal-scorer who has spent his career shuttling between the north-east and London—first with Newcastle for over 200 league appearances and 81 goals, then to West Ham (120 appearances, 47 goals), home to Sunderland (90 appearances, 34 goals) but back to West Ham (107 appearances, 47 goals) before, in the close season in 1979, again being transferred to Sunderland.

35.   A Mixed-up Draw

The football fans in an office were eagerly awaiting the quarter-final draw for the Scottish Cup. Unfortunately there was either a new boy working the teleprinter machine or there was something wrong with the machine because you can see below how the "draw" came out. However, someone soon realised that all the letters of each club had been printed, only their order was wrong. The fans soon sorted things out—can you?

Danebeer   v. Tomorn

Aptrick Lettish   v. Kycleband

Ticcel   v. Ray Untied

Transrear   v. Lowhelmert

Cherbin Ticy   v. Gerrans

Mandorbut   v. Hinebairn

Rhora Rivets   v. Listborn Ailing

Neddue   v. Malkickorn

36. European Club Badges—2

Can you name the six European clubs (and their countries) whose badges are shown below? Here are some clues to help you—in the 1979/80 season, two were beaten by Celtic in the Champion Clubs Cup; two were beaten by Glasgow Rangers in the Cup Winners Cup; whilst of the remaining two, one beat and one lost to Scottish clubs in the U.E.F.A. Cup.

A

B

C

D

E

F

37. Spearheads

In the grid below, fill in the names of players who earned their places in the history of football as goal-scorers—the spearheads of attacks.
Clues to their identities are given opposite.

1. The only player to score a hat-trick in a World Cup Final.

2. The converted wing-half who scored ten goals for Luton against Bristol Rovers in a Third Division (South) match.

3. The player who set up the Football League goal-scoring record of 60 goals in a season in 1927/28.

4. One of today's regular goal-scorers, most of them for Southampton, with the high, present-day tally of 21 goals in 44 (plus two as sub.) matches for England.

5. In 1935 he scored 7 goals in a match for Arsenal—the First Division record.

6. Better known today as the manager of the 1979 European club champions but, until injury prematurely ended his career, a prolific post-war goal-scorer.

7. His 220 League goals for Tottenham and 44 goals for England in the 1960s reflect his uncanny ability to convert the half-chances into goals.

8. England's most-capped player and leading scorer with 49 goals in Full International matches.

9. Supermac—top scorer for England in a Wembley international with five goals against Cyprus in April 1975.

10. For one season his 59 goals (in only 37 matches) was a Football League record until the player at No. 3 above went one better—59 remains the Second Division record for a season.

38. A Man with an Important Job

Below are set out ten clues to the identity of someone with a very important job in football today. See how quickly, starting from clue No. 1 and working downwards, you can name him.

1. He was born in Burnley in 1922 and was thus a bit too young to have established himself as a professional footballer before the war started.

2. He did sign for Chelsea in 1940 as an amateur player, and, during the war, whilst serving in the R.A.F., made guest appearances for Belfast Celtic, Hull City and Bradford Park Avenue.

3. Signed for Bradford Park Avenue (they were then members of the Football League) in 1945 but moved to Brentford in 1949.

4. Re-joined Chelsea in 1952 and had made 21 First Division appearances in Chelsea's 1955 Football League Championship-winning team before being transferred to Fulham for whom he made over 300 appearances before retiring as a player in 1956.

5. Whilst still a Brentford player he was one of the "pioneers" who attended the first F.A. coaching course to be held at Lilleshall.

6. Gained coaching experience with the Oxford University team and the amateur club Walthamstow Avenue before becoming manager of Eastbourne United.

7. Had his first experience of management of a Football League club as the assistant to George Swindin at Highbury.

8. Earlier he had managed the England Youth team and now the England national team manager, Walter Winterbottom, invited him to manage the national Under-23 team.

9. In 1961 he became the manager-coach of West Ham United.

10. And, if you still have not realised who he is, he followed Don Revie as England's national team manager with winning, first the European Championship, and then the 1982 World Cup Competition his targets.

Time for a breather in an international match at Wembley whilst two injured players were being treated in the goalmouth. Who are these two England players? One of them is an established world-class player; the other is at the beginning of his international career.

Pictured are three players – all of them are wearing the strip of clubs new to them in the 1979/80 season. Can you name the players and their new and previous clubs?

Hands are important to goalkeepers – one keeper is
showing his hands to the camera; one comfortably
holds the ball poised for a one-handed throw; but what
has the smiling keeper done to the ball in a
London derby match? Can you name these three
keepers?

A feature of recent seasons has been the matches between Liverpool and Nottingham Forest. Can you name the two contending players in **(1)** and the individual players at **(2)** and **(3)**?

What's the point? **(1)** The player in the middle looks a bit guilty! Who is he and the two players pointing towards him? Who are the two gesticulating players shown at **(2)** and **(3)**?

All Smiles! **(1)** Can you name these three happy Scots? What trophy are they holding? **(2)** Who is this joyful scorer in a Cup-tie? **(3)** A delightful picture of two former club-mates now in opposition but still able to share their enjoyment in playing football. Who are they?

(1) Whoops! The strip and the No.7 will help you name the white-shirted player – and here's a clue to help you name the other player: he is a Scot and plays for Nottingham Forest. **(2)** and **(3)** are Irishmen – one of them making another come-back. Can you name them and their clubs in 1979/80 season?

It's Goals that Count – whether (as **(1)**) scored on a firm Wembley pitch in August or (as **(2)**) on a muddy one in Belfast in October. Who are the players with arms raised in **(1)** and for whom were they playing? Who are the kneeling and squatting pair of players in **(2)**? They were then club-mates but for whom were they playing in the pictured match?

47. Last Season in the European Club Competitions

The 1979/80 season was a poor one for British clubs in the UEFA Cup—a competition that, since its beginning in 1972, had been won three times by English clubs. But we did better in the two major competitions—the Champion Clubs Cup and the Cup-Winners Cup.

1. Whilst the British clubs faltered, one European country dominated the UEFA Cup and provided all four semi-finalists. Which country? How many of the four semi-finalists can you name?

2. Which Turkish club did Arsenal beat in the First Round of the Cup-Winners Cup?

3. Glasgow Rangers in the same competition, after playing in a Preliminary Round, were drawn in the First Round against the West German club, Fortuna Dusseldorf. With what result?

4. There are four rounds, each contested on the two-legged basis, before the Final in both the Champion Clubs and the Cup-Winners Cups, what, up to and including the semi-final stage, did Arsenal in the Cup-Winners and Nottingham Forest in the Champion Clubs have in common?

5. Which club knocked Liverpool out of the Champion Clubs Cup in the First Round?

6. Celtic gained a 2–0 victory over the "old masters", Real Madrid, in the first-leg of the Third Round (the quarter-final) of the Champion Clubs Cup. What was the result in the second leg?

7. Who was the sole survivor of their 1967 European Champion Clubs Cup winning team to play for Celtic in last season's competition?

8. Nottingham Forest, the holders, reached the semi-final of the Champion Clubs Cup by beating Dynamo Berlin 3–1 in Berlin after losing the first leg 0–1 at Nottingham. Who scored Nottingham Forest's three goals in Berlin?

C

48. Young England and the U-21 Championship

1. In the first competition (1976/78) for the European Under-21 Championship, England were defeated in the semi-finals by the eventual champions. Who were they?

2. How many over-age players can a country include in their team in an Under-21 European Championship match?

3. England's opening match in the second (1978/80) European Under-21 Championship was against Denmark in Copenhagen. Who were the two black players in England's team and which of them scored in England's 2–1 victory?

4. Who were the scorers in England's 3–1 win in Bulgaria in an Under-21 Championship match in June 1979?

5. England made certain of qualifying for the quarter-finals when they defeated Denmark 1–0 at Watford in September 1979. Who was the player with the local club who was in England's team?

6. In their final match in the qualifying competition the England Under-21 team beat Bulgaria 5–0 at Leicester in November 1969. How many of the five new "caps" in the England team can you name?

7. Who scored a hat-trick in that 5–0 win over the young Bulgarians?

8. Scotland also qualified for the Under-21 Championship quarter-finals and were drawn against England. The first leg was played at Coventry. Who were the two players in Scotland's team from the Coventry club?

9. England's two central defenders in both legs of the quarter-final tie against Scotland in the European Under-21 Championship came from the same club. Can you name them and their club?

10. What was the result of the quarter-final tie against Scotland played at Coventry (first leg) and Aberdeen (second leg)?

49. True to Form in Italy

Goals have seldom been plentiful in Italian First Division matches and the results of the matches listed below that were played in March 1980 were typical so far as goals were concerned.

In the eight matches, ten goals were scored, with two the most that any side scored—the only three sides that did this were all playing at home. Nine of the sixteen clubs failed to score—four of them in the only drawn matches, those played at Bologna and Naples. Three other home sides failed to score, whilst the away clubs, Cagliari and Perugia, also failed to score. In the local derby matches, Roma won by the odd goal in three whilst a single goal gave Inter their victory.

From the above information can you complete the scores of the matches?

Bologna	....	Ascoli	....
Catanzaro	....	Fiorentina	....
Roma	....	Lazio	....
Milan	....	Inter	....
Napoli	....	Juventus	....
Pescara	....	Cagliari	....
Torino	....	Perugia	....
Udinese	....	Avellino	....

50. Big Money Transfers

The names of two footballers are coded in this diagram—one of bygone days and one of today. Can you solve the code—name the two players and say what "milestones" were reached by their transfers? Do you also know between which two clubs in each case the transfer of registration of the player was transacted?

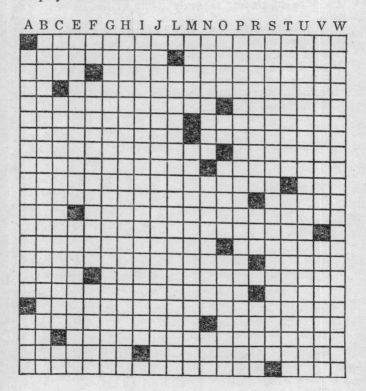

51.   Who Am I?

Can you find the surname of the well-known footballer in this little rhymed puzzle?

> My first is in BREAD but not in LEAD;
>
> My second is in FRED but not in TED.
>
> My third is in SONG but not in SING;
>
> My fourth is in DONG but not in DING.
>
> My fifth is in KNIGHT but not in LORD;
>
> My sixth is in FIGHT but not in SWORD.
>
> My seventh is in NAB but not in STAB;
>
> My last is in GRAB but not in JAB.

Can you also say for which London club I have always played?

52. Eight Scottish Stars of Today

There are clues below to enable you to fill in the names on this grid (using, of course, the letter supplied in its correct order) of eight players who have appeared for Scotland in recent seasons.

1. Cool, elegant Liverpool central defender.
2. Left-back with more than 300 appearances for Manchester City.
3. The most-capped Scottish goalkeeper.
4. Busy midfield player – first with West Bromwich, then Manchester City, briefly Nottingham Forest before going to Everton.
5. Liverpool bought him from Celtic in August 1977 after Kevin Keegan had been transferred to Hamburg.
6. Tricky, typically Scottish winger, transferred from Aberdeen to Leeds. Made first Scottish appearance as substitute in September 1977 but missed the 1978 World Cup matches.
7. Came to Tottenham straight from school but could not settle in London and joined Middlesbrough where he was first capped before joining Liverpool.
8. Strongly-built centre-forward who probably makes more goals than he scores. Moved to Manchester United from Leeds in November 1977.

53. A Close Finish

With one match each to play, the position at the top of the First Division of the first four clubs was as follows:—

	P	W	D	L	F	A	Pts.
Bruddersford	41	27	8	6	76	28	62
Mawne United	41	25	11	5	75	27	61
Knype	41	24	12	5	80	33	60
Milbury Town	41	26	8	7	72	26	60

To add to the excitement, the four clubs in their final match had to play against each other in the following two fixtures:—

Milbury Town v. Mawne United
Knype   v. Bruddersford

1. There was one result that, irrespective of the result of the Milbury-Mawne match, was certain to give Bruddersford the championship. What was it?

2. If Bruddersford drew their match and Mawne won theirs, who would be the champions?

3. If Knype beat Bruddersford 1–0 and Milbury and Mawne drew theirs 3–3, who would be the champions?

4. If Knype beat Bruddersford 1–0 by what score (or scores) would (a) Mawne have to beat Milbury, or (b) Milbury have to beat Mawne?

5. If the Knype-Bruddersford match was drawn, could Milbury become champions? If so, by what result and score?

6. Finally—the four fictional names I have used for the clubs were used by authors in novels—the first three are adult novels in which football is incidentally featured, the last one in two juvenile novels about football. How many of the novels and their authors do you know?

54. Last and First Relay

In this puzzle you must move round the grid in a clockwise direction from the start. The answers to the clues give the names of 14 clubs in the order they have been entered in the puzzle. Each name ends in a lightly shaded square and that last letter of one name becomes the first letter of the next club.

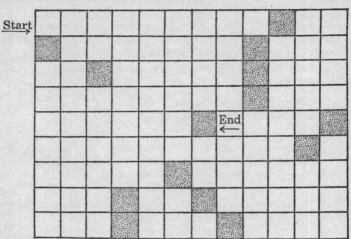

Start →

End ←

1. They transferred Andy Gray to Wolves. (Two words.)
2. Highbury is home to them.
3. Up for the Kop!
4. Twice winners of the European Fairs Cup (1968 and 1971).
5. Down in the Dell!
6. The Magpies of the north-east.
7. The second club to win the Football League Championship.
8. Canaries who used to play at the Nest.
9. Mike Smith became their manager in January 1980.
10. You'll find them at Filbert Street.
11. Today fans nickname them "The Royals" but their fathers would have called them "The Biscuitmen".
12. In their earliest years they were called New Brompton.
13. Wilf Mannion was their most capped player.
14. The first club to win the Football League Championship three seasons in succession.

55.   Not Long Ago

Managers often have to remind their players to forget the
matches they have recently played and to concentrate on
winning the next match. In a similar way even the most
enthusiastic football fans sometimes have difficulty (and
arguments!) in remembering the winners of quite recent
seasons. Here is a test for you to tackle. Without the aid of
reference books, see how many of the champions of the
various divisions of the Football League and the Scottish
League you can correctly enter in the chart below.

Season ending *Football League* First Division	1977	1978	1979
Second Division			
Third Division			
Fourth Division			
Scottish League Premier Division			
First Division			
Second Division			

56. A Busy International Night

On 17th October, 1979, England, Northern Ireland, the Republic of Ireland, Scotland and Wales were all in action in European Football Championship qualifying competition matches.

1. Two of the matches ended with the score 5–1. Which two matches?

2. One of the five countries dropped a point at home. Which of them and against whom?

3. Which country won their home match 3–0? Against whom?

4. Football League clubs supplied 49 of the 55 players who lined-up at the start of the matches. Which two clubs supplied the most players?

5. There were three "Home" Scots in the Scottish line-up at the kick-off—one each from Glasgow Rangers, Partick Thistle and St. Mirren. Can you name them?

6. The Republic of Ireland had two "Home" players in their side—both from Shamrock Rovers. Who were they?

7. Who was the only player in the England team not with an English club?

8. Swansea were the Football League club who supplied most players to the Welsh side—four of them. Who were they?

9. Wales made two substitutions. One of them had not been born in Wales and, in relation to his birthplace, there was a special significance in his appearance in the match. What was it?

10. Northern Ireland's substitute was their only player from an Irish League club. Who was he? And what was his club?

57. The Soccer Bowl

The most important trophy in North American "soccer" is the Soccer Bowl – awarded to the season's overall champions of the NASL. Study the clues below and enter the answers in the puzzle.

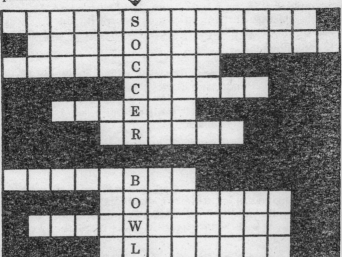

1. What is the name of the ground where the 1979 Soccer Bowl final was played on 8th September?
2. Who was the one-time Ipswich player who scored the two goals for the winners?
3. The winners were from Vancouver. What is the second of the two words of the club's name? Vancouver is the first name of course.
4. The previous season's champions were the New York .... Can you complete the name?
5. On their way to the championship, Vancouver had to defeat the club from Los Angeles. What word completes *their* name?
6. Who was the famous Dutch footballer, once also of Barcelona, in the Los Angeles team?
7. The beaten finalists were the Rowdies. From where?
8. Can you name the Dallas club also beaten by Vancouver?
9. Who was the former England goalkeeper who coached Vancouver?
10. Who was the England 1966 World Cup player who captained Vancouver?

58. Almost the Same

There are always several players with the same surname amongst the professional footballers with Football League clubs—Andy Gray, Frank Gray and Eddie Gray for example, but in the puzzle below you have to find the pairs of players with surnames the same except for one letter as, for example, goalkeeper Parkes (West Ham) and striker Parker (Barnsley).

1. (a) A consistent goal-scorer in recent years for Newcastle, Sunderland (twice), and West Ham United (twice).
   (b) One of Burnley's "transfers-out"—to Everton in August 1974 for £300,000.

2. (a) The veteran Norwich City goalkeeper.
   (b) Twice in recent seasons the European Footballer of the Year.

3. (a) The ginger-haired little "dynamo" who so inspired England in extra-time in the 1966 World Cup Final.
   (b) A later addition to England's midfield whose great career with Manchester City was prematurely ended by injury.

4. (a) Long-standing Bradford City back who was born in the West Indies.
   (b) Regular England player in the middle 1970s when with Derby County. Then, after a spell at Goodison Park, a key member of the 1979/80 Birmingham side.

5. (a) A Leicester-born goalkeeper who is approaching his 500th Football League match appearance. Now with Nottingham Forest after playing for Leicester and Stoke.
   (b) One of Manchester City's many buys during the 1979/80 season—from Wrexham after he had played previously for Cambridge United and Walsall.

6. (a) Another goalkeeper—he made nearly 200 League match appearances for West Ham before being transferred to Orient for the 1979/80 season.
   (b) Strong man in Leicester's defence—born in Sutton Coldfield.

59. The World Cup Winners

Can you fill in the names of the winners of the World Cup in the years between 1930 and 1978 inclusive? To help you, the names of the six winners (some have been successful on more than one occasion) are hidden in the grid below and you can find them by moving from the start-square, one square at a time in any direction, without, however, crossing another square. Every letter is used and used once only.

	R	U	G	A	N	
START → U	Y	A	U	M	Y	B
W	E	G	E	R	A	R
S	T	L	I	Z	I	N
T	I	G	E	N	T	A
A	L	R	L	G	N	E
	Y	A	A	N	D	

1930 ....
1934 ....
1938 ....
1950 ....
1954 ....
1958 ....
1962 ....
1966 ....
1970 ....
1974 ....
1978 ....

60. Names that can Mislead

One could be excused for expecting Mike England, the popular Spurs' player of a few seasons ago, to have been an English international player. But was he? Below are listed a number of international players whose names are misleading in respect of their nationality. Can you say for which of the British "four" countries they played?

Britton	..	..	..	....
English	..	..	..	....
England	..	..	..	....
Francis	..	..	..	....
Norman	..	..	..	....
Poland	..	..	..	....
L. Scott (Arsenal)	..		..	....
E. Scott (Liverpool)	..		..	....
Wales ..	..	..	..	....
M. Walsh (Q.P.R.)	..		..	....
I. Walsh (Crystal Palace)		..		....
E. Welsh (Carlisle)	..		..	....
R. C. Welsh (Old Harrovians)				....

In recent seasons several names of foreign extraction have appeared on the team sheets of British international teams. For which of the "home" countries have these players played in international matches?

Krzywicki	..	..	..	....
Macari	..	..	..	....
Nardiello	..	..	..	....
Pejic ..	..	..	..	....
Viljoen	..	..	..	....

61. Find the Scorer

Black, White, Green and Gray are the four front-line players in the attacking team. But, as you can see, often their way to goal is blocked—by tackles when there is a line across the path; by the ball going into touch or over the goal-line. But one of them has got the ball in the net. How quickly can you discover the scorer?

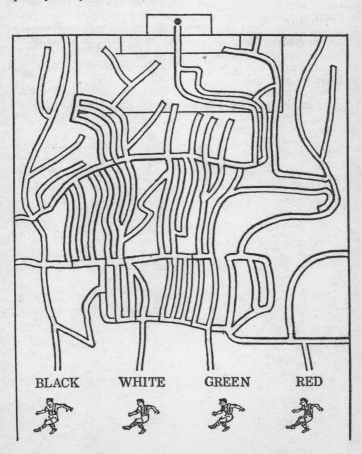

BLACK   WHITE   GREEN   RED

62.   A Line-up Puzzle

By using the letters from the columns shown opposite you
can fill in on the diagram the names of the players in a team
that won an exciting match at Wembley in 1979. The team
is shown in 4–3–3 formation starting from the goalkeeper.
The last name is that of the substitute who came on late in
the game. A black square marks the end of each name and
some names run on from one line to the next. The letters
making up the names are shown *directly below* the appro-
priate squares but are not in any special order. (The name
of the 'keeper, in other words, starts with any one of the
letters shown in the first column—Y, C, O, R or J.) Each
letter is used but is only used once—so cross through each
letter as you use it.

When you have discovered the team, can you name the
club and remember what was the exciting match they won?

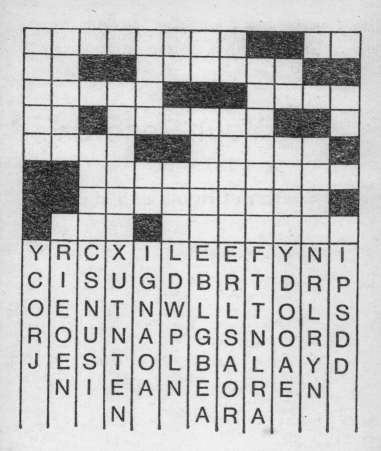

D

For Your Records

1979—80

The Season at Home and in Europe

FOOTBALL LEAGUE—DIVISION ONE

	P	Home W	D	L	F	A	Away W	D	L	F	A	Pts
LIVERPOOL	42	15	6	0	46	8	10	4	7	35	22	60
Manchester Untd.	42	17	3	1	43	8	7	7	7	22	27	58
Ipswich Town	42	14	4	3	43	13	8	5	8	25	26	53
Arsenal	42	8	10	3	24	12	10	6	5	28	24	52
Nottingham For.	42	16	4	1	44	11	4	4	13	19	32	48
Wolverhampton	42	9	6	6	29	20	10	3	8	29	27	47
Aston Villa	42	11	5	5	29	22	5	9	7	22	28	46
Southampton	42	14	2	5	53	24	4	7	10	12	29	45
Middlesbrough	42	11	7	3	31	14	5	5	11	19	30	44
West Brom. Alb.	42	9	8	4	37	23	2	11	8	17	27	41
Leeds United	42	10	7	4	30	17	3	7	11	16	33	40
Norwich City	42	10	8	3	38	30	3	6	12	20	36	40
Crystal Palace	42	9	9	3	26	13	3	7	11	15	37	40
Tottenham Hot.	42	11	5	5	30	22	4	5	12	22	40	40
Coventry City	42	12	2	7	34	24	4	5	12	22	42	39
Brighton & Hove	42	8	8	5	25	20	3	7	11	22	37	37
Manchester City	42	8	8	5	28	25	4	5	12	15	41	37
Stoke City	42	9	4	8	27	26	4	6	11	17	32	36
Everton	42	7	7	7	28	25	2	10	9	15	26	35
Bristol City	42	6	6	9	22	30	3	7	11	15	36	31
Derby County	42	9	4	8	36	29	2	4	15	11	38	30
Bolton Wand.	42	5	11	5	19	21	0	4	17	19	52	25

F.A. CUP FINAL

West Ham United (Brooking)	1	Arsenal	0

FOOTBALL LEAGUE—DIVISION TWO

		Home					Away					
	P	W	D	L	F	A	W	D	L	F	A	Pts
LEICESTER C.	42	12	5	4	32	19	9	8	4	26	19	55
Sunderland	42	16	5	0	47	13	5	7	9	22	29	54
Birmingham City	42	14	5	2	37	16	7	6	8	21	22	53
Chelsea	42	14	3	4	34	16	9	4	8	32	36	53
Queen's Park R.	42	10	9	2	46	25	8	4	9	29	28	49
Luton Town	42	9	10	2	36	17	7	7	7	30	28	49
West Ham Untd.	42	13	2	6	37	21	7	5	9	17	22	47
Cambridge Untd.	42	11	6	4	40	23	3	10	8	21	30	44
Newcastle Untd.	42	13	6	2	35	19	2	8	11	18	30	44
Preston N. End	42	8	10	3	30	23	4	9	8	26	29	43
Oldham Athletic	42	12	5	4	30	21	4	6	11	19	32	43
Swansea City	42	13	1	7	31	20	4	8	9	17	33	43
Shrewsbury Town	42	12	3	6	41	23	6	2	13	19	30	41
Orient	42	7	9	5	29	31	5	8	8	19	23	41
Cardiff City	42	11	4	6	21	16	5	4	12	20	32	40
Wrexham	42	13	2	6	26	15	3	4	14	14	34	38
Notts County	42	4	11	6	24	22	7	4	10	27	30	37
Watford	42	9	6	6	27	18	3	7	11	12	28	37
Bristol Rovers	42	9	8	4	33	23	2	5	14	17	41	35
Fulham	42	6	4	11	19	28	5	3	13	23	46	29
Burnley	42	5	9	7	19	23	1	6	14	20	50	27
Charlton Athletic	42	6	6	9	25	31	0	4	17	14	47	22

FOOTBALL LEAGUE CUP FINAL

Wolverhampton Wanderers 1   Nottingham Forest 0
(Gray)

FOOTBALL LEAGUE—DIVISION THREE

		Home					Away					
	P	W	D	L	F	A	W	D	L	F	A	Pts
GRIMSBY TN.	46	18	2	3	46	16	8	8	7	27	26	62
Blackburn Rovers	46	13	5	5	34	17	12	4	7	24	19	59
Sheffield Wed.	46	12	6	5	44	20	9	10	4	37	27	58
Chesterfield	46	16	5	2	46	16	7	6	10	25	30	57
Colchester United	46	10	10	3	39	20	10	2	11	25	36	52
Carlisle United	46	13	6	4	45	26	5	6	12	21	30	48
Reading	46	14	6	3	43	19	2	10	11	23	46	48
Exeter City	46	14	5	4	38	22	5	5	13	22	46	48
Chester	46	14	6	3	29	18	3	7	13	20	39	47
Swindon Town	46	15	4	4	50	20	4	4	15	21	43	46
Barnsley	46	10	7	6	29	20	6	7	10	24	36	46
Sheffield United	46	13	5	5	35	21	5	5	13	25	45	46
Rotherham Untd.	46	13	4	6	38	24	5	6	12	20	42	46
Millwall	46	14	6	3	49	23	2	7	14	16	36	45
Plymouth Argyle	46	13	7	3	39	17	3	5	15	20	38	44
Gillingham	46	8	9	6	26	18	6	5	12	23	33	42
Oxford United	46	10	4	9	34	24	4	9	10	23	38	41
Blackpool	46	10	7	6	39	34	5	4	14	23	40	41
Brentford	46	10	6	7	33	26	5	5	13	26	47	41
Hull City	46	11	7	5	29	21	1	9	13	22	48	40
Bury	46	10	4	9	30	23	6	3	14	15	36	39
Southend United	46	11	6	6	33	23	3	4	16	14	35	38
Mansfield Town	46	9	9	5	31	24	1	7	15	16	34	36
Wimbledon	46	6	8	9	34	38	4	6	13	18	43	34

WELSH CUP FINAL (Played in two legs)

Newport County (Tynan 2)	2	Shrewsbury Town (Moore o.g.)	1
Shrewsbury Town	0	Newport County (Tynan, Lowndes, Gwyther)	3

FOOTBALL LEAGUE—DIVISION FOUR

	P	W	D	L	F	A	W	D	L	F	A	Pts
		Home						**Away**				
HUDDERS-FIELD TOWN	46	16	5	2	61	18	11	7	5	40	30	66
Walsall	46	12	9	2	43	23	11	9	3	32	24	64
Newport County	46	16	5	2	47	22	11	2	10	36	28	61
Portsmouth	46	15	5	3	62	23	9	7	7	29	26	60
Bradford City	46	14	6	3	44	14	10	6	7	33	36	60
Wigan Athletic	46	13	5	5	42	26	8	8	7	34	35	55
Lincoln City	46	14	8	1	43	12	4	9	10	21	30	53
Peterborough U.	46	14	3	6	39	22	7	7	9	19	25	52
Torquay United	46	13	7	3	47	25	2	10	11	23	44	47
Aldershot	46	10	7	6	35	23	6	6	11	27	30	45
Bournemouth	46	8	9	6	32	25	5	9	9	20	26	44
Doncaster Rovers	46	11	6	6	37	27	4	8	11	25	36	44
Northampton T.	46	14	5	4	33	16	2	7	14	18	50	44
Scunthorpe Untd.	46	11	9	3	37	23	3	6	14	21	52	43
Tranmere Rovers	46	10	4	9	32	24	4	9	10	18	32	41
Stockport Cnty.	46	9	7	7	30	31	5	5	13	18	41	40
York City	46	9	6	8	35	34	5	5	13	30	48	39
Halifax Town	46	11	9	3	29	20	2	4	17	17	52	39
Hartlepool	46	10	7	6	36	28	4	3	16	23	36	38
Port Vale	46	8	6	9	34	24	4	6	13	22	46	36
Hereford United	46	8	7	8	22	21	3	7	13	16	31	36
Darlington	46	7	11	5	33	26	2	6	15	17	48	35
Crewe Alexandra	46	10	6	7	25	27	1	7	15	10	41	35
Rochdale	46	6	7	10	20	28	1	6	16	13	51	27

SCOTTISH LEAGUE—PREMIER DIVISION

		Home					Away					
	P	W	D	L	F	A	W	D	L	F	A	Pts
ABERDEEN	36	10	4	4	30	18	9	6	3	38	18	48
Celtic	36	13	3	2	44	17	5	8	5	17	21	47
St. Mirren	36	11	5	2	37	23	4	7	7	19	26	42
Dundee United	36	9	7	2	23	6	3	6	9	20	24	37
Rangers	36	11	5	2	29	16	4	2	12	21	30	37
Greenock Morton	36	9	4	5	24	16	5	4	9	27	30	36
Partick Thistle	36	6	8	4	24	22	5	6	7	19	25	36
Kilmarnock	36	7	6	5	19	19	4	5	9	17	33	33
Dundee	36	9	3	6	33	30	1	3	14	14	43	26
Hibernian	36	6	4	8	23	31	0	2	16	6	36	18

(*Note.* In the Scottish League Premier Division each club
plays *four* times against the other nine clubs. In both the
First and Second Divisions each club plays *three* times
against the other thirteen clubs.)

SCOTTISH CUP FINAL

Celtic   1   Rangers   0
(McCluskey)   (after extra time)

SCOTTISH LEAGUE CUP FINAL

Aberdeen   0   Dundee United   0
(Played at Hampden Park, Glasgow)   (after extra time)

Dundee United   3   Aberdeen   0
(Pettigrew 2, Sturrock)
(Replay at Dens Park, Dundee F.C's ground.)

SCOTTISH LEAGUE—DIVISION ONE

| | | Home | | | | | | Away | | | | |
	P	W	D	L	F	A	W	D	L	F	A	Pts
HEARTS	39	13	6	1	33	18	7	7	5	25	21	53
Airdrieonians	39	14	2	4	46	21	7	7	5	32	26	51
Ayr United	39	11	5	4	37	22	5	7	7	27	29	44
Dumbarton	39	10	4	5	34	22	9	2	9	25	29	44
Raith Rovers	39	8	7	5	30	22	6	8	5	29	24	43
Motherwell	39	9	7	3	32	17	7	4	9	27	31	43
Hamilton Acad.	39	11	5	3	39	20	4	5	11	21	39	40
Stirling Albion	39	7	6	7	23	19	6	7	6	17	21	39
Clydebank	39	9	6	5	32	21	5	2	12	26	36	36
Dunfermline	39	7	7	5	23	24	4	6	10	16	33	35
St. Johnstone	39	5	5	9	28	32	7	5	8	29	42	34
Berwick Rangers	39	5	8	7	36	31	3	7	9	21	33	31
Arbroath	39	7	5	7	31	32	2	5	13	19	47	28
Clyde	39	3	6	10	22	34	3	7	10	21	35	25

SCOTTISH LEAGUE—DIVISION TWO

| | | Home | | | | | | Away | | | | |
	P	W	D	L	F	A	W	D	L	F	A	Pts
FALKIRK	39	11	7	2	34	12	8	5	6	31	23	50
East Stirling	39	10	3	6	28	20	11	4	5	27	20	49
Forfar Athletic	39	9	6	5	35	27	10	2	7	28	24	46
Albion Rovers	39	11	5	3	46	21	5	7	8	27	35	44
Queens Park	39	8	5	6	32	21	8	4	8	27	26	41
Stenhousemuir	39	10	1	8	32	22	6	8	6	24	29	41
Brechin City	39	9	4	6	35	23	6	6	8	26	36	40
Cowdenbeath	39	9	7	4	33	24	5	5	9	21	28	40
Montrose	39	8	5	7	37	35	6	5	8	23	28	38
East Fife	39	9	6	5	26	21	3	3	13	19	36	33
Stranraer	39	7	4	8	26	25	5	4	11	25	40	32
Meadowbank T.	39	7	2	11	17	29	5	6	8	25	41	32
Queen of the Sth.	39	6	6	8	29	29	5	3	11	22	40	31
Alloa Athletic	39	8	4	7	32	28	3	3	14	12	36	29

EUROPEAN CHAMPION CLUBS' CUP

Preliminary Round

Dundalk (Republic of Ireland)	1	Linfield (N. Ireland)	1
Linfield	0	Dundalk	2

(Played in Haarlem, Holland)

First Round

Liverpool (England)	2	Dynamo Tbilisi (USSR)	1
Dynamo Tbilisi	3	Liverpool	0
Arges Pitesti (Rumania)	3	AEK Athens (Greece)	0
AEK Athens	2	Arges Pitesti	0
Levski Spartak (Bulgaria)	0	Real Madrid (Spain)	1
Real Madrid	2	Levski Spartak	0
Valur FC (Iceland)	0	Hamburg SV (W. Ger.)	3
Hamburg SV	2	Valur FC	1
Servette FC (Switzerland)	3	Beveren SK (Belgium)	1
Beveren SK	1	Servette FC	1
Vejle BK (Denmark)	3	Austria Memphis Wien (Austria)	2
Austria Memphis Wien	1	Vejle BK	1
Nottingham Forest (Eng.)	2	Oesters IF Vaxjo (Sweden)	0
Oesters IF Vaxjo	1	Nottingham Forest	1
FC Porto (Portugal)	0	Milan AC (Italy)	0
Milan AC	0	FC Porto	1
Red Boys Differdange (Luxembourg)	2	Omonia Nicosia (Cyprus)	1
Omonia Nicosia	6	Red Boys Differdange	1
Hajduk Split (Yugoslavia)	1	Trabzonspor (Turkey)	0
Trabzonspor	0	Hajduk Split	1
Dundalk	2	Hibernians (Malta)	0
Hibernians	1	Dundalk	0
IK Start (Norway)	1	RC Strasbourg (France)	2
RC Strasbourg	4	IK Start	0
Partizani (Albania)	1	Glasgow Celtic (Scotland)	0
Glasgow Celtic	4	Partizani Tirana	1
Helsingin JK (Finland)	1	Ajax Amsterdam (Netherlands)	8
Ajax Amsterdam	8	Helsingin JK	1
Ujpest Dozsa (Hungary)	3	Dukla Prague (Czechoslovakia)	2
Dukla Prague	2	Ujpest Dozsa	0

First Round (cont)

Dynamo Berlin (E. Ger.)	4	Ruch Chorzow (Poland)	1
Ruch Chorzow	0	Dynamo Berlin	0

Second Round

Hamburg SV	3	Dynamo Tbilisi	1
Dynamo Tbilisi	2	Hamburg SV	3
Glasgow Celtic	3	Dundalk	2
Dundalk	0	Glasgow Celtic	0
FC Porto	2	Real Madrid	1
Real Madrid	1	FC Porto	0
Vejle BK	0	Hajduk Split	3
Hadjuk Split	1	Vejle BK	2
Ajax Amsterdam	10	Omonia Nicosia	0
Omonia Nicosia	4	Ajax Amsterdam	0
Dynamo Berlin	2	Servette FC	1
Servette FC	2	Dynamo Berlin	2
Dukla Prague	1	RC Strasbourg	0
RC Strasbourg	2	Dukla Prague	0
(after extra time)			
Nottingham Forest	2	Arges Pitesti	0
Arges Pitesti	1	Nottingham Forest	2

Third Round (Quarter-Finals)

Nottingham Forest	0	Dynamo Berlin	1
Dynamo Berlin	1	Nottingham Forest	3
Celtic	2	Real Madrid	0
Real Madrid	3	Celtic	0
Hamburg SV	1	Hajduk Split	0
Hajduk Split	3	Hamburg SV	2
Racing Strasbourg	0	Ajax Amsterdam	0
Ajax Amsterdam	4	Racing Strasbourg	0

Semi-Finals

Nottingham Forest	2	Ajax Amsterdam	0
Ajax Amsterdam	1	Nottingham Forest	0
Real Madrid	2	Hamburg SV	0
Hamburg SV	5	Real Madrid	1

Final—28th May, 1980, in Madrid

Nottingham Forest	1	Hamburg SV	0
(Robertson)			

EUROPEAN CUP WINNERS CUP

Preliminary Round

BK 1903 Copenhagen (Denmark)	6	Apoel Nicosia (Cyprus)	0
Apoel Nicosia	0	BK 1903 Copenhagen	1
Glasgow Rangers (Scot.)	1	Lillestrom SK (Norway)	0
Lillestrom SK	0	Glasgow Rangers	2

First Round

Sliema Wanderers (Malta)	2	Boavista Porto (Portugal)	1
Boavista Porto	8	Sliema Wanderers	0
Glasgow Rangers	2	Fortuna Dusseldorf (W. Germany)	1
Fortuna Dusseldorf	0	Glasgow Rangers	0
Juventus (Italy)	2	Raba Vasas Eto Gyor (Hungary)	0
Raba Vasas Eto Gyor	2	Juventus	1
Panionios (Greece)	4	FC Twente Enschede (Netherlands)	0
FC Twente Enschede	3	Panionios	1
Arka Gdynia (Poland)	3	Beroe Stara Zagora (Bulgaria)	2
Beroe Stara Zagora	2	Arka Gdynia	0
Wrexham (Wales)	3	FC Magdeburg (E. Ger.)	2
FC Magdeburg	5	Wrexham	2
		(after extra time)	
Young Boys Bern (Switzerland)	2	Steaua Bucharest (Rumania)	2
Steaua Bucharest	6	Young Boys Bern	0
Lahden Reipas (Finland)	0	Aris Bonnevoie (Lux.)	1
Aris Bonnevoie	1	Lahden Reipas	0
Swarovski Innsbruck (Austria)	1	Lokomotive Kosice (Czechoslovakia)	2
Lokomotive Kosice	1	Swarovski Innsbruck	0
Beerschot (Belgium)	0	NK Rijeka (Yugoslavia)	0
NK Rijeka	2	Beerschot	1
BK 1903 Copenhagen	2	Valencia (Spain)	2
Valencia	4	BK 1903 Copenhagen	0
Arsenal (England)	2	Fenerbahce (Turkey)	0
Fenerbahce	0	Arsenal	0

IFK Gothenburg (Sweden)	1	Waterford (Rep. of Ireland)	0
Waterford	1	IFK Gothenburg	1
Cliftonville (N. Ireland)	0	FC Nantes (France)	1
FC Nantes	7	Cliftonville	0
IA Akranes (Iceland)	0	Barcelona (Spain)	1
Barcelona	5	IA Akranes	0

Dynamo Moscow (Soviet Union) qualified when Vlaznia Shkoder (Albania) refused to play.

Second Round

Arsenal	2	FC Magdeburg	1
FC Magdeburg	2	Arsenal	2
Aris Bonnevoie	1	Barcelona	4
Barcelona	7	Aris Bonnevoie	1
Panionios	1	IFK Gothenburg	0
IFK Gothenburg	2	Panionios	0
Lokomotive Kosice	2	NK Rijeka	0
NK Rijeka	3	Lokomotive Kosice	0
FC Nantes	3	Steaua Bucharest	2
Steaua Bucharest	1	FC Nantes	2
Dynamo Moscow	0	Boavista Porto	0
Boavista Porto	1	Dynamo Moscow	1
Beroe Stara Zagora	1	Juventus	0
Juventus	3	Beroe Stara Zagora	0
Valencia	1	Glasgow Rangers	1
Glasgow Rangers	1	Valencia	3

Third Round (Quarter-Finals)

Arsenal	5	Gothenburg	1
Gothenburg	0	Arsenal	0
Dynamo Moscow	0	FC Nantes	2
FC Nantes	2	Dynamo Moscow	3
Rijeka	0	Juventus	0
Juventus	2	Rijeka	0
Barcelona	0	Valencia	1
Valencia	4	Barcelona	3

Semi-Finals

Arsenal	1	Juventus	1

Semi-Finals (cont)

Juventus	0	Arsenal	0
FC Nantes	2	Valencia	1
Valencia	4	FC Nantes	0

Final—16th May, 1980, in Brussels

Arsenal	0	Valencia	0

(after extra time)

VALENCIA won on penalties 5–4.

U.E.F.A. CUP

First Round

Glenavon (N. Ireland)	0	Standard Liege (Belgium)	1
Standard Liege	1	Glenavon	0
Lokomotiv Sofia (Bulgaria)	3	Ferencvaros (Hungary)	0
Ferencvaros	2	Lokomotiv Sofia	0
Real Sporting Gijon (Spain)	0	PSV Eindhoven (Netherlands)	0
PSV Endhoven	1	Real Sporting Gijon	0
Sporting Portugal (Port.)	2	Bohemians (Rep. Ireland)	0
Bohemians	0	Sporting Portugal	0
Zbrojovka Brno (Czechoslovakia)	6	Esbjerg (Denmark)	0
Esbjerg	1	Zbrojovka Brno	1
Bohemians (Czechoslovakia)	0	Bayern Munich (West Germany)	2
Bayern Munich	2	Bohemians	2
Galatasaray (Turkey)	0	Red Star Belgrade (Yugoslavia)	0
Red Star Belgrade	3	Galatasaray	1
SK Rapid Wien (Austria)	0	Diosgyor Miskolc (Hungary)	1
Diosgyor Miskolc	3	SK Rapid Wien	2
Internazionale Milan (Italy)	3	Real San Sebastian (Spain)	0
Real San Sebastian	2	Internazionale Milan	0
Atletico Madrid (Spain)	1	Dynamo Dresden (E. Germany)	2
Dynamo Dresden	3	Atletico Madrid	0
Valetta FC (Malta)	0	Leeds United (England)	4
Leeds United	3	Valetta FC	0
Perugia AC (Italy)	1	Dynamo Zagreb (Yugoslavia)	0
Dynamo Zagreb	0	Perugia AC	0
Aris Salonika (Greece)	3	Benfica (Portugal)	1
Benfica	2	Aris Salonika	1
FC Zurich (Switzerland)	1	FC Kaiserslautern (W. Germany)	3
FC Kaiserslautern	5	FC Zurich	1

First Round (cont)

Widzew Lodz (Poland)	2	AS St. Etienne (France)	1
AS St. Etienne	3	Widzew Lodz	0
Skeid (Norway)	1	Ipswich Town (England)	3
Ipswich Town	7	Skeid	0
Kalmar FF (Sweden)	2	Keflavik (Iceland)	1
Keflavik	1	Kalmar FF	0
Bor. Monchengladbach (W. Germany)	3	Viking Stavanger (Norway)	0
Viking Stavanger	1	Bor. Monchengladbach	1
Dundee United (Scotland)	0	Anderlecht (Belgium)	0
Anderlecht	1	Dundee United	1
Aarhus (Denmark)	1	Stal Mielec (Poland)	1
Stal Mielec	0	Aarhus	1
Carl Zeiss Jena (E. Germany)	2	West Bromwich Albion (England)	0
West Bromwich Albion	1	Carl Zeiss Jena	2
Kuopion Pallotoverit (Finland)	1	Malmo FF (Sweden)	2
Malmo FF	2	Kuopion Pallotoverit	0
Aberdeen (Scotland)	1	Eintracht Frankfurt (W. Germany)	1
Eintracht Frankfurt	1	Aberdeen	0
Feijenoord (Netherlands)	1	Everton (England)	0
Everton	0	Feijenoord	1
Naples (Italy)	2	Olympiakos (Greece)	0
Olympiakos	1	Naples	0
Shakhter Donetz (Soviet Union)	2	Monaco (France)	1
Monaco	2	Shakter Donetz	0
Dynamo Bucharest (Rumania)	3	Alki Larnaca (Cyprus)	0
Alki Larnaca	0	Dynamo Bucharest	9
Dynamo Kiev (Soviet Union)	2	CSKA Sofia (Bulgaria)	1
CSKA Sofia	1	Dynamo Kiev	1
Orduspor (Turkey)	2	Banik Ostrava (Czechoslovakia)	0
Banik Ostrava	6	Orduspor	0
Wiener SC (Austria)	0	Universitatea Craiova (Rumania)	0
Universitatea Craiova	3	Weiner SC	1

First Round (cont)

VfB Stuttgart (W. Germany)	1	AC Torino (Italy)	0
AC Torino	2	VfB Stuttgart	1

(after extra time)

Progres Niedercorn (Luxembourg)	0	Grasshopper (Switzerland)	2
Grasshopper	4	Progres Niedercorn	0

Second Round

Dundee United	0	Diosgyor Miskolc	1
Diosgyor Miskolc	3	Dundee United	1
Bor. Monchengladbach	1	Internazionale Milan	1
Internazionale Milan	2	Bor. Monchengladbach	3

(after extra time)

Aarhus	1	Bayern Munich	2
Bayern Munich	3	Aarhus	1
Red Star Belgrade	3	Carl Zeiss Jena	2
Carl Zeiss Jena	2	Red Star Belgrade	3
Grasshopper	0	Ipswich	0
Ipswich	1	Grasshopper	1
Zbrojovka Brno	3	Keflavik	1
Keflavik	1	Zbrojovka Brno	2
PSV Eindhoven	2	AS St. Etienne	0
AS St. Etienne	6	PSV Eindhoven	0
Sporting Portugal	1	FC Kaiserslautern	1
FC Kaiserslautern	2	Sporting Portugal	0
Aris Salonika	1	Perugia AC	1
Perugia AC	0	Aris Salonika	3
Universitatea Craiova	2	Leeds United	0
Leeds United	0	Universitatea Craiova	2
Dynamo Dresden	1	VfB Stuttgart	1
VfB Stuttgart	0	Dynamo Dresden	0
Banik Ostrava	1	Dynamo Kiev	0
Dynamo Kiev	2	Banik Ostrava	0
Dynamo Bucharest	2	Eintracht Frankfurt	0
Eintracht Frankfurt	3	Dynamo Bucharest	0

(after extra time)

Lokomotiv Sofia	4	Monaco	2
Monaco	2	Lokomotiv Sofia	1
Standard Liege	2	Naples	1
Naples	1	Standard Liege	1

Second Round (cont)

Feijenoord	4	Malmo FF	0
Malmo FF	1	Feijenoord	1

Third Round

Diosgyor Miskolc	0	FC Kaiserslautern	2
FC Kaiserslautern	6	Diosgyor Miskolc	1
Grasshopper	0	VfB Stuttgart	2
VfB Stuttgart	3	Grasshopper	0
Bor. Monchengladbach	2	Universitatea Craiova	0
Universitatea Craiova	1	Bor. Monchengladbach	0
Lokomotiv Sofia	1	Dynamo Kiev	0
Dynamo Kiev	2	Lokomotiv Sofia	1
Eintracht Frankfurt	4	Feijenoord	1
Feijenoord	1	Eintracht Frankfurt	0
Bayern Munich	2	Red Star Belgrade	0
Red Star Belgrade	3	Bayern Munich	2
AS St. Etienne	4	Aris Salonika	1
Aris Salonika	3	AS St. Etienne	3
Standard Liege	1	Zbrojovka Brno	2
Zbrojovka Brno	3	Standard Liege	2

Fourth Round (Quarter-Finals)

St. Etienne	1	B. Monchengladbach	4
B. Monchengladbach	2	St. Etienne	0
F.C. Kaiserslautern	1	Bayern Munich	0
Bayern Munich	4	F.C. Kaiserslautern	1
VfB Stuttgart	3	Lokomotiv Sofia	1
Lokomotiv Sofia	0	VfB Stuttgart	1
Eintracht Frankfurt	4	Zbrojovka Brno	1
Zbrojovka Brno	3	Eintracht Frankfurt	2

Semi-Finals

Bayern Munich	2	Eintracht Frankfurt	0
Eintracht Frankfurt	5	Bayern Munich	1
VfB Stuttgart	2	B. Monchengladbach	1
B. Monchengladbach	2	VfB Stuttgart	0

Final—played in two legs (home and away)

B. Monchengladbach (Kulik 2, Matthaus)	3	Eintracht Frankfurt (Karger, Holzenbein)	2
Eintracht Frankfurt (Cha)	1	B. Monchengladbach	0

EINTRACHT FRANKFURT won on away goals.

1980-81—THE IMPORTANT FIXTURES

August 1980

Sat.   9 F.A. Charity Shield Match at Wembley
          Football League Cup First Round (1st leg)
          Scottish League season begins
Wed. 13 Football League Cup First Round (2nd leg)
Sat.   16 *Football League Season begins*
Wed. 27 Football League Cup Second Round (1st leg)

September

Wed.   3 Football League Cup Second Round (2nd leg)
Tues. 9 Sweden v Scotland (U.E.F.A. Under-21)
Wed. 10 ENGLAND v NORWAY (World Cup Qual.)
          SWEDEN v SCOTLAND (World Cup Qual.)
          REP. of IRELAND v NETHERLANDS (World
          Cup Qual.)
Wed. 17 European Champion Clubs Cup First Round
          (1st leg)
          European Cup-Winners Cup First Round (1st
          leg)
          U.E.F.A. Cup First Round (1st leg)
Wed. 24 Football League Cup Third Round

October

Wed.   1 European Champion Clubs Cup First Round
          (2nd leg)
          European Cup-Winners Cup First Round (2nd
          leg)
          U.E.F.A. Cup First Round (2nd leg)
Tues. 14 Rumania v England (U.E.F.A. Under-21)
Wed. 15 RUMANIA v ENGLAND (World Cup Qual.)
          SCOTLAND v PORTUGAL (World Cup Qual.)
          N. IRELAND v SWEDEN (World Cup Qual.)
          WALES v TURKEY (World Cup Qual.)
          REP. of IRELAND v BELGIUM (World Cup
          Qual.)
Wed. 22 European Champion Clubs Cup Second Round
          (1st leg)
          European Cup-Winners Cup Second Round (1st
          leg)
          U.E.F.A. Cup Second Round (1st leg)
Tues. 28 FRANCE v REP. of IRELAND (World Cup
          Qual.)
Wed. 29 Football League Cup Fourth Round

November

Wed.   5   European Champion Clubs Cup Second Round
            (2nd leg)
            European Cup-Winners Cup Second Round (2nd
            leg)
            U.E.F.A. Cup Second Round (2nd leg)
Tues. 18   England v Switzerland (U.E.F.A. Under-21)
            Scotland v Denmark (U.E.F.A. Under-21)
Wed.   19   ENGLAND v SWITZERLAND (World Cup
            Qual.)
            PORTUGAL v N. IRELAND (World Cup
            Qual.)
            WALES v CZECHOSLOVAKIA (World Cup
            Qual.)
            REP. of IRELAND v CYPRUS (World Cup
            Qual.)
Sat.   22   F.A. Challenge Cup First Round
Wed.   26   U.E.F.A. Cup Third Round (1st leg)

December

Wed.   3   Football League Cup Fifth Round
Wed.   10   U.E.F.A. Cup Third Round (2nd leg)
Sat.   13   F.A. Challenge Cup Second Round
            Scottish Cup First Round

January 1981

Sat.   3   F.A. Challenge Cup Third Round
            Scottish Cup Second Round
Wed.   14   Football League Cup Semi-Finals (1st leg)
Sat.   24   F.A. Challenge Cup Fourth Round
            Scottish Cup Third Round

February

Wed.   11   Football League Cup Semi-Finals (2nd leg)
Sat.   14   F.A. Challenge Cup Fifth Round
            Scottish Cup Fourth Round
Wed.   25   ISRAEL v SCOTLAND (World Cup Qual.)

March

Wed.   4   European Champion Clubs Cup Quarter-Finals
            (1st leg)
            European Cup-Winners Cup Quarter-Finals (1st
            leg)
            U.E.F.A. Cup Quarter-Finals (1st leg)

Sat.	7	F.A. Challenge Cup Sixth Round
		Scottish Cup Fifth Round
Sat.	14	FOOTBALL LEAGUE CUP FINAL
Wed.	18	European Champion Clubs Cup Quarter-Finals (2nd leg)
		European Cup-Winners Cup Quarter-Finals (2nd leg)
		U.E.F.A. Cup Quarter-Finals (2nd leg)
Wed.	25	ENGLAND v SPAIN (Friendly Full International)
		SCOTLAND v N. IRELAND (World Cup Qual.)
		TURKEY v WALES (World Cup Qual.)
		BELGIUM v REP. of IRELAND (World Cup Qual.)
		Spain v England ('B' International)

April

Wed.	8	European Champion Clubs Cup Semi-Finals (1st leg)
		European Cup-Winners Cup Semi-Finals (1st leg)
		U.E.F.A. Cup Semi-Finals (1st leg)
Sat.	11	F.A. Challenge Cup Semi-Finals
		Scottish Cup Semi-Finals
Wed.	22	European Champions Clubs Cup Semi-Finals (2nd leg)
		European Cup-Winners Cup Semi-Finals (2nd leg)
		U.E.F.A. Cup Semi-Finals (2nd leg)
Tues.	28	England v Rumania (U.E.F.A. Under-21)
Wed.	29	ENGLAND v RUMANIA (World Cup Qual.)
		N. IRELAND v PORTUGAL (World Cup Qual.)
		SCOTLAND v ISRAEL (World Cup Qual.)

May

Sat.	2	*Football League season ends*
		Scottish League season ends
Wed.	6	U.E.F.A. CUP FINAL (1st leg)
Sat.	9	F.A. CHALLENGE CUP FINAL
		SCOTTISH CUP FINAL
Wed.	13	EUROPEAN CUP-WINNERS CUP FINAL

Sat.	16	N. IRELAND v ENGLAND (B.H.C.)
		WALES v SCOTLAND (B.H.C.)
Tues.	19	ENGLAND v WALES (B.H.C.)
		SCOTLAND v N. IRELAND (B.H.C.)
Wed.	20	U.E.F.A. CUP FINAL (2nd leg)
Fri.	22	N. IRELAND v WALES (B.H.C.)
Sat.	23	ENGLAND v SCOTLAND (B.H.C.)
Wed.	27	EUROPEAN CHAMPION CLUBS CUP FINAL
Sat.	30	SWITZERLAND v ENGLAND (World Cup Qual.)
		WALES v SOVIET UNION (World Cup Qual.)
Sun.	31	Switzerland v England (U.E.F.A. Under-21)

June

Wed.	3	SWEDEN v N. IRELAND (World Cup Qual.)
Fri.	5	Hungary v England (U.E.F.A. Under-21)
Sat.	6	HUNGARY v ENGLAND (World Cup Qual.)

ANSWERS TO PUZZLES

1. A. (a) Universitatea Craiova, Rumania, (b) Leeds United, (c) UEFA Cup, (d) Universitatea won. B. FC Arges Pitesti, Rumania, (b) Nottingham Forest, (c) Champion Clubs Cup, (d) Arges lost. C. (a) Skeid, Norway, (b) Ipswich Town, (c) UEFA Cup, (d) Skeid lost. D. (a) Oesters IF Vaxjo, Sweden, (b) Nottingham Forest, (c) Champion Clubs Cup, (d) Vaxjo lost. E. (a) Carl Zeiss Jena, East Germany, (b) West Bromwich Albion, (c) UEFA Cup, (d) Jena won. F. (a) Valetta FC, Malta, (b) Leeds United, (c) UEFA Cup, (d) Valetta lost.

2. 1. Manchester United. 2. Crystal Palace. 3. Jimmy Greaves. 4. Billy Wright. 5. Peterborough United. 6. Sam Bartram. 7. The Hawthorns. 8. Bob Paisley. 9. Exeter City and Newcastle United. 10. (a) Torquay United. (b) Chester (c) Brighton. 11. John Charles. 12. Ian Callaghan.

3. 1. Rimmer. 2. Clemence. 3. Hodge. 4. Burridge. 5. Shilton. 6. Sealey.

4. 1. Luton Town. 2. Walsall. 3. Sheffield United. 4. Arsenal. 5. Stoke City. 6. Northampton Town. 7. Wimbledon. 8. Aldershot. 9. Tottenham Hotspur. 10. Wolverhampton Wanderers. 11. West Ham United. 12. Southampton who were founded as St. Mary's.

5. 1. Coppell. 2. Barnes. 3. Keegan. 4. Shilton. 5. Watson. 6. Channon. 7. Woodcock.

6. Petar Borota to Chelsea from Partisan, Yugoslavia; Ivan Golac to Southampton from Partisan, Yugoslavia; Dave Watson to Werder Bremen from Manchester City, England (later returned to sign for Southampton); Frans Thijssen to Ipswich from Twente Enschede, Holland; Arnold Muhren to Ipswich from Twente Enschede, Holland; Ricardo Villa to Tottenham Hotspur from Racing, Argentina; Kevin Keegan to Hamburg from Liverpool, England; Alex Sabella to Sheffield United from River Plate, Argentina; Kazimierz Deyna to Manchester City from Legia Warsaw, Poland; Osvaldo Ardiles to Tottenham Hotspur from Huracan, Argentina; and Laurie Cunningham to Real Madrid from West Bromwich Albion, England.

7. 1950 Williams (England). 1954 Merrick (England), Martin (Scotland); 1958 McDonald (England), Younger

and Brown (Scotland). 1962 Springett (England). 1966 Banks (England). 1970 Banks and Bonetti (England). 1974 Harvey (Scotland). 1978 Rough (Scotland).

8.

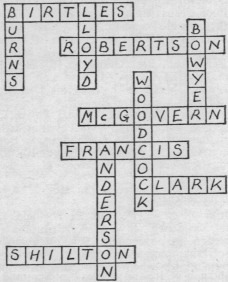

9. 1. Bob Cumming for Grimsby against Exeter. 2. The match between Wolverhampton Wanderers and Liverpool. Wolverhampton asked for a postponement because their ground alterations were not completed and the Football League, after an initial refusal, agreed in view of the large attendance expected for the visit of Liverpool. 3. Arsenal. 4. (a) Justin Fashanu, (b) Garth Crooks. 5. Gordon Davies. 6. Portsmouth in their 6th match when they were beaten by Tranmere. 7. (a) Crystal Palace beaten in their 10th match by Southampton, (b) Walsall beaten in their 14th match by Halifax. 8. Brighton won by 1–0 and remarkably this was Brighton's first-ever win away from home in the First Division. 9. David Fairclough. 10. Steve Moran.

10. You do not award a goal. Law X of the game is quite clear that "a goal is scored when *the whole of the ball* has passed over the goal-line between the goal-posts and under the cross-bar" (my italics). In the drawing you will see that the 'keeper has stopped the ball before the whole of it had passed over the line. It is important to always remember that "the space within the inside areas of the field of play *includes* the width of the lines marking these areas."

11. Las Palmas 4 Atletico Madrid 2; Athletic Bilbao 4 Seville 3; Valencia 2 Malaga 1; Rayo Vallecano 5 Burgos 2; Barcelona 0 Gijon 0; Almeria 2 Hercules 0; Zaragoza 0 Real Sociedad 2; Betis 2 Salamanca 0; Real Madrid 2 Espanol 0.

12. Kevin Keegan.

13. 1. Phil Parkes from Queen's Park Rangers to West Ham. 2. Kevin Hird from Blackburn to Leeds. 3. (a) David Mills, (b) Terry Cochrane. 4. (a) Steve Whitworth, (b) Steve Sims. 5. (a) Micky Thomas, (b) Joey Jones. 6. (a) Gordon Smith, (b) Neil McNab. 7. Peter Eastoe from Q.P.R. and Micky Walsh from Everton. 8. Tadeusz Nowak. 9. Terry Curran. 10. Brian Kidd.

14. Aston Villa and Liverpool are the two clubs. Aston Villa have won the FA Cup more times than any other club; Liverpool the Football League Championship.

15. 1. Win against Bulgaria (3–0), draw with Sweden (0–0), lost to Austria (3–4). 2. The 75th Anniversary of the Swedish F.A. 3. England and Wales—England beat Scotland and N. Ireland; Wales beat Scotland but drew with N. Ireland. The match between England and Wales was drawn. 4. Kenny Sansom of Crystal Palace and Laurie Cunningham. 5. Kevin Keegan. 6. Kevin Keegan who had to return to West Germany for Hamburg's next match. 7. (a) Glen Hoddle. (b) Kevin Reeves. 8. The Republic of Ireland. 9. (a) Steve Coppell. (b) Ron Healey. 10. Against the Republic of Ireland (1–1) in Dublin.

16. A. Club Always Ready, La Paz, Bolivia. B. The Strongest also of La Paz, Bolivia. C. Bohemians, Prague, Czechoslovakia. (The kangaroo badge was adopted when Bohemians were the first Czechoslovakian side to tour Australia.) D. 1st. Vienna Football Club, Vienna, Austria. (Austrians, of course, call their capital city Wien, but the club retains the English version, Vienna.) E. Sporting Boys Association, Lima, Peru. F. Young Boys, Bern, Switzerland.

17. False. Barnes, Coppell and Latchford were newcomers but Wilkins had first played in May 1976—also against Italy in New York. 2. True—a draw against Everton was followed by defeats against Manchester City, Aston Villa and Queen's Park Rangers, and a draw against Bristol City. 3. False—Peters is not the only one. Mick Channon has also scored over 20 goals for England. 4. False—in addition to those four clubs, Liverpool did this in 1906. 5. True—they lost for the first time at Coventry in their 20th match. 6. True—David Peach and Nick Holmes were the survivors. 7. False—the next international after Keegan to go to West Germany was Dave Watson to Werder Bremen. He soon returned to Southampton. 8. True—Bristol City in 1907, Oldham in 1915 and Charlton in 1937. None of them have ever won the Championship.

18. The sentence reads: "Can you name the present managers of the England and Scotland national teams and say who were the managers they succeeded?" The answer is: Ron Greenwood (England) and Jock Stein (Scotland) succeeded Don Revie and Ally McLeod respectively.

19. 1. Middlesbrough. 2. Grimsby Town. 3. Reading. 4. Blackburn Rovers. 5. Walsall. 6. Everton. 7. Cardiff City. 8. Tranmere Rovers. 9. Sunderland. 10. Newport County. 11. Wigan Athletic. 12. Port Vale.

20. A. Czechoslovakia. Blue in the triangle, white top, red bottom. B. West Germany. From the top—black, red and yellow. C. Italy. From the left—green, white and red. D. Spain. From the top—red, yellow, red.

21. 1. North American Soccer League. 2. Across the Hudson River from New York at East Rutherford in the state of New Jersey. 3. Two—the advantage to the Football League clubs is the saving on their wages bill. 4. Detroit Express. 5. (a) Ian Greaves then manager of Bolton Wanderers. (b) Frank Worthington. 6. (a) Southampton. (b) Washington Diplomats. 7. Dennis Tueart. 8. (a) Fort Lauderdale Strikers. (b) New York Cosmos. (c) Minnesota Kicks.

22. 1. Watson. 2. Cowans. 3. Dalglish. 4. Latchford. 5. Boyer. 6. Coppell.

23. 1. Glen Hoddle. 2. Charlie George. 3. Pedro Verde. 4. (a) Jim Arnold to Blackburn Rovers. (b) Billy

Kellock to Peterborough United. 5. John Mahoney, he and John Toshack are cousins. 6. (a) Jimmy Dickinson. (b) Roy Sproson. (c) John Trollope. (d) Terry Paine. 7. Ron Harris of Chelsea. 8. Kevin Keegan.

24. In alphabetical order: Arsenal, Chelsea, Derby County, Everton, Ipswich Town, Leeds United, Liverpool, Manchester United, Nottingham Forest, Southampton, Sunderland, West Ham United.

25. *From A to Z the countries read:* Argentina, Brazil, Italy, Poland, Iran, West Germany, Tunisia, Austria, Mexico, France, Argentina, Brazil, Scotland, Netherlands (Holland), Austria, Hungary, Peru, Netherlands (Holland), Scotland, Poland, Spain, West Germany, Sweden, Italy.

26. Aberdeen 1 Partick Thistle 1; Dundee 1 Dundee United 1; Kilmarnock 1 St. Mirren 1; Morton 0 Celtic 1; Rangers 1 Hibernian 0.

27. Kevin Keegan, Hamburg; Tony Woodcock, Cologne; Laurie Cunningham, Real Madrid. This was the first time that an England team had included three players from foreign clubs.

28. 1. Ray Clemence for Liverpool. 2. Brian Clough. 3.

David Johnson. 4. Arthur Rowley. 5. Alan Hansen. 6. Bob Houghton. 7. Trevor Francis. 8. John Toshack. 9. William Ralph "Dixie" Dean. 10. Mike Smith.

29. 1. Dundee United. 2. St. Mirren. 3. Falkirk. 4. Celtic. 5. Dunfermline Ath. 6. Aberdeen. 7. Kilmarnock. 8. Hibernian. 9. Dundee United. 10. Dumbarton. 11. Morton. 12. St. Mirren. 13. Glasgow Rangers. 14. Hibernian. 15. Aberdeen.

30. This was the FA Cup Third Round match when Halifax beat Manchester City 1–0. The teams were: *Halifax* (left on the teams sheet)—Kilner, Dunleavy, Hutt, Evans, Harris, Hendrie, Firth, Kennedy, Mountford, Smith and Stafford. *Manchester City*—Corrigan, Ranson, Power, Reid, Caton, Bennett, Henry, Daley, Robinson, Viljoen and Shinton.

31. 1. Herbert Chapman—Huddersfield Town and Arsenal; Brian Clough—Derby County and Nottingham Forest. 2. Only 16—the three mentioned against Aston Villa and one each against 13 other clubs. On 28 occasions Clemence and Co. kept a clean sheet. 3. (a) Jack Charlton, (b) Billy Bremner, (c) Allan Clarke. The connection is that they were all members of Don Revie's successful Leeds United team. 4. Alan Curtis. 5. Laurie Cunningham. 6. The reigning champions Liverpool beat the FA Cup-holders Arsenal 3–1. 7. Dundee United. 8. Billy Bingham. 9. Mike England. 10. Geoff Hurst.

32. 1. (a) Aston Villa beat Colchester, (b) Sunderland beat Newcastle. 2. (a) Queen's Park Rangers, (b) Bristol City. 3. Grimsby. 4. (a) Altrincham, (b) Barking. 5. Harlow Town. 6. (a) Chester, (b) Wigan. 7. (a) Liverpool, (b) Swindon Town. 8. Watford. 9. Ray Stewart for West Ham United. 10. Andy Gray for Wolverhampton Wanderers.

33. No, you should not be satisfied but must get the game started again correctly. Law VIII headed "The Start of Play" states that: "The Referee having given a signal, the game shall be started by a player taking a place-kick (i.e. a kick at the ball while it is stationary on the ground in the centre of the field of play) *into his opponents' half* of the field of play." (My italics.)

In the drawing you will see that the place-kick did not send the ball into the opponents' half of the field.

What in fact should, and usually does, happen, if this sort of opening move is intended, is that the centre-forward taps the ball *forward* to a team-mate standing beside him, and that player, once the whole of the ball has crossed the halfway line, can pass the ball back.

34. 1. Mick Channon. 2. Leighton James. 3. Tommy Taylor. 4. Tony Kellow. 5. Martin Dobson. 6. Alan Buckley. 7. Bryan "Pop" Robson.

35. Aberdeen v Morton; Partick Thistle v Clydebank; Celtic v Ayr United; Stranraer v Motherwell; Brechin City v Rangers; Dumbarton v Hibernian; Raith Rovers v Stirling Albion; Dundee v Kilmarnock.

36. A. Dundalk, Republic of Ireland (lost to Celtic). B. Lillestrom, Norway (lost to Rangers). C. Eintracht Frankfurt, West Germany (beat Aberdeen). D. Anderlecht, Belgium (lost to Dundee United). E. Fortuna Dusseldorf, West Germany (lost to Rangers). F. Partizani Tirana, Albania (lost to Celtic).

37. 1. Hurst. 2. Payne. 3. Dean. 4. Channon. 5. Drake. 6. Clough. 7. Greaves. 8. Charlton. 9. MacDonald. 10. Camsell.

38. Ron Greenwood.

39. Bryan Robson of West Bromwich (in his first Full International match for England—against the Republic of Ireland) and Kevin Keegan.

40. 1. Emlyn Hughes in Wolves strip after his transfer from Liverpool. 2. Stuart Pearson for West Ham United after his transfer from Manchester United. 3. Mike Robinson for Manchester City after his transfer from Preston N.E.

41. 1. Gary Bailey (Manchester United). 2. Barry Daines (Tottenham Hotspur). 3. Pat Jennings (Arsenal).

42. 1. Trevor Francis (Nottingham Forest) and Alan Hansen (Liverpool). 2. Gary Birtles (Nottingham Forest). 3. Ray Kennedy (Liverpool).

43. 1. Willie Young (Arsenal) in the middle, Chris Jones (Spurs) left of picture and David O'Leary (Arsenal). 2. Tony Currie (QPR). 3. Duncan McKenzie (Blackburn Rovers).

44. 1. Graeme Souness, Alan Hansen and Kenny Dalglish of Liverpool holding the Charity Shield. 2. Keith Bertschin for Birmingham. 3. Keeper Joe Corrigan (Manchester City) and Mike Channon (Southampton).

45. 1. White-shirted Ardiles of Spurs climbing over Kenny Burns. 2. George Best playing for Hibernian. 3. Liam Brady of Arsenal—pictured playing for the Republic of Ireland.

46. 1. Terry McDermott (the scorer) and behind him Kenny Dalglish—playing for Liverpool against Arsenal in the 1979 Charity Shield match. (2) Trevor Francis (kneeling) and Tony Woodcock who has just scored his first goal for England in the course of England's 5–1 win over N. Ireland.

47. 1. West Germany. Bayern Munich, Eintracht Frankfurt. Borussia Monchengladbach. VfB Stuttgart. 2. Fenerbahce. 3. Rangers won—2–1 at home and 0–0 away. 4. Each of them were drawn to play the first leg at home in every round. 5. Dynamo Tbilisi. 6. Real Madrid won 3–0 to take the tie with the aggregated score of 3–2. 7. Bobby Lennox. 8. Trevor Francis two of them and John Robertson the third from the penalty spot.

48. 1. Yugoslavia. 2. Two. 3. Bob Hazell (then with Wolves) and Cyrille Regis (WBA). It was the defender Hazell who scored. England's second goal was scored by Glenn Hoddle. 4. Regis 2 and Robson. 5. Luther Blissett. 6. Birtles (Nottingham Forest), Crooks (Stoke), Hilaire (Crystal Palace), Dennis (Birmingham) and Ranson (Manchester City). The first two named were the over-age players in the team. 7. Garth Crooks. 8. Andy Blair and Gary Gillespie. 9. Terry Butcher and Russell Osman of Ipswich Town. 10. England won the tie — 2–1 at Coventry and 0–0 at Aberdeen.

49. Bologna 0 Ascoli 0; Catanzaro 0 Fiorentina 1; Roma 2 Lazio 1; Milan 0 Inter 1; Napoli 0 Juventus 0; Pescara 2 Cagliari 0; Torino 2 Perugia 0; Udinese 0 Avellino 1.

50. Alf Common and Trevor Francis. Common's transfer in 1905 from Sunderland to Middlesbrough was the first to reach four figures—£1,000. Francis's in February 1979 from Birmingham to Nottingham Forest was the first between British clubs to top a million pounds (including the Football League levy and the deductible VAT).

51. Brooking of West Ham United.

52. 1. Hansen. 2. Donachie. 3. Rough. 4. Hartford. 5. Dalglish. 6. Graham. 7. Souness. 8. Jordan.

53. 1. If Bruddersford won their match they woul
ended the season with 64 points, more than
Mawne or Milbury could get. 2. Mawne would
champions. With one match to play both Brudd
and Mawne had goal-differences of plus 48. I
dersford drew, their goal-difference was uncha
Mawne won, their goal-difference had to inc
the margin of their victory and so, with both
63 points, Mawne would go in front on goal-d
3. Knype would be the champions. They, Bru
and Mawne would all finish with 62 points.
and Knype would have the same goal-differen
48) but Knype would be champions because th
scored more goals. 4. (a) Any score would give l
the championship since they would have 63 poi
Knype's 62. (b) Milbury would have to beat Maw
at least three clear goals (3–0, 4–1, 5–2 etc) to incr
their goal-difference to plus 49 as compared to Kny
plus 48 (and a greater number of goals scored su
that if Milbury only won by any two-goals marg
although their goal-difference would be the same a
Knype's the latter's greater number of goals would be
decisive). 5. It would not be possible for Milbury to be
champions because Bruddersford would have totalled
63 points—one more than it was possible for Milbury
to get. 6. Bruddersford in J. B. Priestley's *Good Com-
panions*; Mawne United in Francis Brett Young's *The
Black Diamond*; Knype in Arnold Bennett's *The Card*
(and in other stories of the Five Towns); Milbury Town,
if you will forgive me, in my two juvenile football
novels, *On the Ball* and *Up the Town*.

54. 1. Aston Villa. 2. Arsenal. 3. Liverpool. 4. Leeds.
5. Southampton. 6. Newcastle. 7. Everton. 8. Norwich.
9. Hull. 10. Leicester. 11. Reading. 12. Gillingham.
13. Middlesbrough. 14. Huddersfield.

55. *Reading down the columns:* 1977—Liverpool, Wolver-
hampton Wanderers, Mansfield, Cambridge United,
Celtic, St. Mirren and Stirling Albion; 1978—Notting-
ham Forest, Bolton, Wrexham, Watford, Glasgow
Rangers, Morton and Clyde; 1979—Liverpool, Crystal
Palace, Shrewsbury, Reading, Celtic, Dundee and
Berwick Rangers.

1. Northern Ireland 1 England 5 and West Germany 5 Wales 1. 2. Scotland against Austria one-all. 3. The Republic of Ireland beat Bulgaria 3—0. 4. Arsenal and Manchester United each supplied six players. Arsenal's were Jennings, Rice, Nelson for N. Ireland, David O'Leary, Brady and Stapleton for the Republic of Ireland. Manchester United's six were wider spread— Steve Coppell and Wilkins for England, Nicholl and McIlroy for N. Ireland, Grimes for the Republic of Ireland, and McQueen for Scotland. (In fact when Micky Thomas came on as substitute for Wales, United had an interest in all five sides!) 5. Jardine (Rangers), Rough (Partick) and Munro (St. Mirren). 6. Mulligan and Pierse O'Leary. 7. Kevin Keegan then with Hamburg. 8. Phillips, Mahoney, James and Toshack. 9. George Berry of Wolves was born in West Germany and the match was being played in Cologne against West Germany. 10. Peter Rafferty of Linfield.

57. 1. Giants Stadium. 2. Trevor Whymark. 3. Whitecaps. 4. Cosmos. 5. Aztecs. 6. Cruyff. 7. Tampa Bay. 8. Tornados. 9. Tony Waiters. 10. Alan Ball.

58. 1. (a) Robson, (b) Dobson; 2. (a) Keelan, (b) Keegan; 3. (a) Ball, (b) Bell; 4. (a) Podd, (b) Todd; 5. (a) Shilton, (b) Shinton; 6. (a) Day, (b) May.

59. 1930 Uruguay, 1934 Italy, 1938 Italy, 1950 Uruguay, 1954 West Germany, 1958 Brazil, 1962 Brazil, 1966 England, 1970 Brazil, 1974 West Germany, 1978 Argentina.

60. Britton (England), English (N. Ireland), England (Wales), Francis (England), Norman (England), Poland (Wales), L. Scott (England), E. Scott (Ireland), Wales (Scotland), M. Walsh (Rep. of Ireland), I. Walsh (Wales), E. Welsh (N. Ireland), R. C. Welsh (England). Krzywicki (Wales), Macari (Scotland), Nardiello (Wales), Pejic (England), Viljoen (England).

61. Green is the goal-scorer.

62. Arsenal's 1979 F.A. Cup-winning team of Jennings; Rice, O'Leary, Young, Nelson; Talbot, Price, Brady; Sunderland, Stapleford, Rix; Walford. The match was exciting because of its final four minutes when, with Arsenal leading 2–0, Manchester United equalised through McQueen and McIlroy, only for Sunderland to regain the lead with a minute left of play.